The Lies That Win

Army Promotions

Attention Authors

The Lies That Win

Army Promotions

Lt. Gen. Raj Kadyan (Retd.)
PVSM, AVSM, VSM

Manas Publications
New Delhi - 110 002 (India)

MANAS PUBLICATIONS
(Publishers, Distributors, Importers & Exporters)
4858, Prahlad Street,
24, Ansari Road, Darya Ganj,
New Delhi - 110 002 (INDIA)
Ph.: (O) 23260783, 23265523; (R) 23842660
Fax: 011- 23272766
E-mail: manaspublications@vsnl.com

ISBN 81-7049-236-X
Rs. 595/-

Typeset by
Manas Publications

Printed in India by
Nice Printing Press, Delhi
and Published by Mrs. Suman Lata for
Manas Publications, 4858, Prahlad Street
24, Ansari Road, Darya Ganj
New Delhi 110002 (INDIA)

Introduction

I retired from the Army after over 40 years of active service. It was a very healthy, happy and satisfying period. However, it was marred by one episode. This is the story of that episode – the most unpleasant and painful episode in an otherwise almost perfect service. I have decided to recount that episode here in this book for two reasons. Firstly, to share some crucial and unknown facts about it with the readers. Secondly, and no less important, to tell my countrymen that they cannot afford to be smug about their defence forces, the last bastion of our nationhood. The corrupt bureaucrats, callous politicians, and pliable military leaders make a deadly combination that can ruin any Army. And our Army will be no exception, unless we do something to stem the rot now.

The story basically relates to the appointment of a General Officer Commanding-in-Chief (GOC-in-C), or, what is popularly known as Army Commander. There was only one vacancy falling to the lot of our batch and as per rules followed without exception almost since Independence, it should have come to me, but it went to a junior, Lt Gen HRS Kalkat, AVSM. This was the only time, before and hence, that it has happened when a qualified and eligible senior was available.

I believe such things happen all the time in civil jobs, but fortunately the Army had largely remained insulated from such interference and extraneous considerations. We need to keep it that way. This book is intended to be a wake-up call in pursuance of that effort.

Contents

1

Promotion System in the Army

The Army has a well-established system of promotions. It was promulgated with the issue of Royal Army Instruction 1937. Since then it has been streamlined and updated to suit the requirements of the Army of an independent country. The updated selection system was issued vide Army Headquarters letter dated 6 May 1987. It is time tested and is as objective as any system managed by human beings can ever be. It is important to know the system being followed.

After the recent abolition of the rank of 2nd Lieutenant, the Army officers have a ladder of nine ranks, listed below, in the ascending order:

- Lieutenant (Lt)
- Captain (Capt)
- Major (Maj)
- Lieutenant Colonel (Lt Col)
- Colonel (Col)
- Brigadier (Brig)

- Major General (Maj Gen)
- Lieutenant General (Lt Gen)
- General (Gen)

These are called ranks. In each rank an officer can be posted to a variety of assignments. These are called appointments (or posts) and are distinct from ranks. These posts may be within the officer's battalion/regiment or on staff, or as an instructor in a training institution, etc.

After being granted permanent commission from the Indian Military Academy, an officer is granted the rank of Lt. Nearly 500 cadets thus get commission every June and every December. At the time of commissioning, based on their overall performance during training as cadets, all officers are placed in an order of merit. His or her position in merit is denoted by the allotment of an Indian Commission (IC) number to each individual officer. (Short Service commissioned officers, passing out of the Officers Training Academy, Chennai, are allotted Short Service or SS numbers. These get changed to IC numbers once an officer is granted regular commission subsequently. This merit placing stays with the officer throughout his service in the Army. As long as any two officers hold the same rank, their IC number determines their inter-se seniority. It is significant to note that no two officers are ever placed or can ever be placed equal in merit.

Promotion from Lt to Capt and Capt to Maj is on a timed schedule subject to an officer passing the prescribed promotion examinations. Thus every officer who passes these examinations is promoted from Lt to Capt and Capt to Maj. Promotion from the rank of Maj to Lt Col and upwards up to the rank of Lt Gen (called select ranks) is through a system of selection done by a selection board. There are thus a total of five selection boards. These are:

(a)	Selection Board No 4	-	For Maj to Lt Col
(b)	Selection Board No 3	-	For Lt Col to Col
(c)	Selection Board No 2	-	For Col to Brig
(d)	Selection Board No 1	-	For Brig to Maj Gen
(e)	Special Selection Board	-	For Maj Gen to Lt Gen

(Note: After this book was drafted, selection for promotion from Maj to Lt Col has been done away with - Author)

The aim of these boards, their composition and guidelines of assessment are spelt out in the Army Headquarters letter dated 6 May, 1987. The duties of the selection boards are given in Paragraph 108 of the Defence Services Regulations, Regulations for the Army, Revised Edition 1987 (In short DSR). The DSR are issued under the authority of the Government of India and cover salient aspects of the administration of the Regular Army. The Preface is signed by the Defence Secretary and clarifies that departmental orders and instructions are based on, and take their authority from, these Regulations. Further, should any variance arise between such orders and instructions and these Regulations, the latter shall prevail. Paragraph 108 of the DSR clearly states that the selection boards will assess officers for promotion from one rank to the next. There are never any selection boards convened to select officers for various appointments/posts within the same rank.

It is noteworthy that the selection boards deal with promotions up to the rank of Lt Gen only. After one reaches the rank of Lt Gen, there is only one more promotion to the rank of Gen. In the entire Army there is only one Gen who holds the post of the Chief of the Army Staff (COAS). The decision as to which officer is to be promoted to the rank of Gen and appointed COAS is entirely the prerogative of the government. No criteria or guidelines for this promotion are laid down beyond saying that the COAS is selected out of the Army Commanders/Vice COAS. In practice, however, the seniormost Lt Gen is generally appointed COAS. Thus, after one reaches the rank of Lt Gen there are no more selection boards.

During their deliberations the members of a selection board take into account a number of factors that constitute the criteria for selection. This criteria for such selection and promotion are given in Army Headquarters letter dated 6 May 1987.

An officer of the rank of Lt Gen, with four other officers as members, chairs the selection board from Maj to Lt Col, Lt Col to Col and Col to Brig. The members may be of the rank of Lt Gen, Maj Gen, or Brig (only for Selection Board No 4). The total number of members, including the chairman, is generally five. An officer of the Military Secretary's (MS) Branch acts as secretary to the board. He is there only to assist in the technical aspects and is not permitted to participate in the deliberations of the board. To add fairness and objectivity to the system the names of the candidate officers are not disclosed to the board members. Instead, a code system is used and the board members only deal with index numbers without knowing either the name of the officer being considered or other personal details that could reveal one's identity.

For promotion from Brig to Maj Gen and Maj Gen to Lt Gen, the COAS himself is the chairman and the Vice COAS and all the Army Commanders are members. The Military Secretary acts as the secretary of the board.

The selection boards base their decision on a number of factors. The main factor, of course, is the grades obtained by an officer in all his annual confidential reports (ACR). This report is written on each officer every year and is endorsed by at least three successive layers in the hierarchy. (Recently, as a modification to this system, for officers up to the eighth year of service there is a performance card instead of an ACR). The first level to write the report is called the initiating officer (IO), the next level is called the reviewing officer (RO) and the next higher level is called the senior reviewing officer (SRO). The IO, the RO and the SRO are also collectively referred to as the reporting officers. An officer may get more than one report in a year in case during the year either he is posted out or his IO is changed. The basic requirement is that to become due for getting a CR the ratee officer must physically serve with the IO for at least 90 days. The ACR form is very elaborate and has a very large number of qualities that are required to be graded by the IO, the RO and the SRO. There are separate forms for different ranks as the traits required at various levels are different.

Up to the rank of Maj Gen there are quantifiable grades to be awarded by the IO, RO and the SRO. These grades are on a scale of 1 to 9. This is essential because officers up to the rank of Maj Gen have to be screened for promotion to the next rank and numerical awards in their various traits permit comparison. In addition to the numerical values in various traits the reporting officers also write a pen picture to describe any special traits that the officer may possess and which are not covered in the prescribed traits for which quantified values have been laid down.

Some portion of the ACR is shown to the ratee officer while other portion—mainly dealing with recommendations for promotions to the next higher rank— is not shown to him. When a ratee officer sees his report, he is required to sign it. (The policy in this regard has been frequently changing between the 'closed' system where no portion of the report is shown to the ratee, and the 'open' system where a part of the report is shown. The 'open' system is presently in vogue). In case, it is not convenient or expedient for a ratee to sign the report in the presence of the IO, the latter sends him a signed extract which the former reads, signs and sends to the Army Headquarters.

The reports written by the RO and the SRO are not shown unless these include some adverse or advisory remarks, in which case it is mandatory for the report to be shown to the ratee.

Once an officer is promoted to the rank of Lt Gen his ACR form does not have numerical grades. This is so because after reaching the rank of Lt Gen there are no more selection boards and there is no need for any comparison. For Lt Gen the form has a simple pen picture and two questions which are to be answered by a yes/no response by the reporting officer. These questions are:

(a) Do you consider him fit in every way to hold his present rank?

(b) Do you consider him fit for promotion to the next higher rank/appointment?

It is significant to note that for Lt Gen the next rank is only of Gen and the only appointment in that next rank is of the COAS. Therefore, in the ACR form for Lt Gen, apart from his ability to hold his present rank, it is his fitness for the rank of Gen and for the appointment of COAS that is being judged and commented upon through answer to question at (b) above. (Note: After I filed the court case in 1998, and obviously as a result of this case, the ACR form for Lt Gen has been slightly modified. However, even in the modified form, there are no numerical values for various traits. The revised form came into use in the year 2000 and is not relevant for the purpose of this book). After a Lt Gen is appointed an Army Commander, no more ACR is written on him. Therefore, fitness for promotion to the rank of Gen and for the appointment of COAS is judged before an officer is appointed an Army Commander; hence the relevance of question at (b) above.

As per existing instructions the IO, RO and SRO are required to include in their assessment both strong as well as weak points of the rated officer. The weak points have to be shown to the officer so that he has an opportunity to improve upon whatever weakness in him has been pointed out as also to represent against these in case he feels that these remarks are not justified. The remarks of a more serious nature are termed adverse remarks while those that are not serious are called advisory remarks. The policy on advisory remarks has been long in existence and was reiterated vide Army Headquarters letter dated 21 October, 1998. While speaking of advisory remarks the letter reads:

> *"...Also human imperfections mean that any officer, however capable, can be advised to improve upon any trait in the quest for excellence. An officer who is clear above average bordering on outstanding can be advised to improve some facet of his personality so that he attains truly outstanding capabilities/ performance. In this context, to treat any advisory remark as 'adverse' would be a travesty of justice and completely off the mark...While adverse remarks are essential to place on record the weaknesses of the ratee, advisory remarks are also needed to bring in further improvements in the ratee's performance and overall development, though per se they may not reflect any trait of the ratee."*

The advisory remarks, as the very name suggests, are in the nature of an advice to the ratee officer to effect and show improvement. In case he takes the advice and improves/ overcomes whatever weakness was pointed out, and such a weakness does not find mention in subsequent reports, these advisory remarks are no longer valid and have no negative effect on future promotions. In fact as per the latest policy of the Army Headquarters (given in their letter dated 21 October 1998 cited above) the advisory remarks are not to be written in the main report. Instead, these are to be pasted on a separate slip. This fully establishes that the advisory remarks have no lasting significance.

The selection boards screen officers of one particular batch. A batch comprises officers commissioned in one calendar year, which generally includes two courses passing out in June and December. Before the board assembles, the MS Branch carries out its own assessment of the officers of the batch under scrutiny. Based on this internal assessment the MS Branch prepares what is called the 'internal batch assessment' where all officers of the batch under question are placed on a merit list. The Army Headquarters policy letter dated 6 May 1987 lays down that in order to ensure objectivity in the selection system, separate assessment by different agencies namely, internal assessment by the MS Branch and assessments by the selection board are taken into account. In case of any variance between the two assessments, the Board is requested to re-examine a particular case. In case the Board still remains committed to its view then the Military Secretary may bring the disparity to the notice of the COAS who takes a final decision. I have mentioned this point to highlight the importance of the internal assessment carried out by the MS Branch.

Before being considered for promotion to the next rank, an officer has to do a laid-down criteria appointment in his present rank. For example, if an officer of the rank of Brig is being considered for promotion to the rank of Maj Gen it is mandatory for him to do a criteria appointment as Brig. The criteria appointment in each rank and the duration for which it should be held is specified. The period spent in the criteria appointment is called 'Adequately Exercised' (AE) period. In practice it is seen that owing to management problem there are a large number of officers who have a shortfall in their AE period at the time of their being considered by the selection board for promotion. This shortfall may invariably be due to the constraints of the system. Therefore, a provision for waiving this shortfall exists and is laid down vide Army Headquarters letter dated 6 May 1986. According to this letter the power to waive the AE period is as under:

(a) MS- Up to three months.

(b) COAS- Period exceeding three months.

Thus relaxation in the time spent in these criteria appointments is entirely within the powers of the COAS.

As laid down in the Army Headquarters letter dated 6 May 1987, the selection boards award any one of the following gradings to an officer being considered for promotion:

'A' – fit for accelerated promotion to the next higher rank.

'B' – Fit for promotion in his turn to the next higher rank.

'Z' – Unfit for promotion to the next higher rank at present.

'D' – Defer consideration till the officer is adequately exercised in criteria appointment.

'W'– Withdrawn cannot be awarded a definite grading due to incomplete documentation, complaints against ACR/disciplinary award and case awaiting decision in legal courts.

From the gradings it is significant to note that a 'D' grading is awarded only on the grounds of inadequate AE, and the power to waive that is vested in the COAS.

Every officer is given three chances for consideration for promotion. When an officer is awarded the grading 'D' it means that the officer would be considered again next time and that would count as his first chance. Whenever such 'deferred' officers are found 'fit' subsequently, they pick up the higher rank and take their original position as per the IC number and there is no loss of seniority vis-à-vis those officers of the batch who had been promoted ahead of them. As opposed to this, an officer who is awarded the grading 'Z' stands to lose seniority. In the event of such an officer being found 'fit' in the second (or third) chance i.e., with the subsequent batches, he becomes junior to all those of his own batch who were found 'fit' in the first chance. He is placed on top of the next (junior) batch with which he is found 'fit'.

For promotions from Maj to Lt Col and from Lt Col to Col, the final authority for approving the recommendations of selection board is vested with the COAS. For the other three boards the final authority is with the Government.

An officer who is graded 'unfit' has the right to file a complaint against his supersession. This complaint can take two forms. It can either be a non-statutory complaint, which means that the final authority to take a decision on this would be the COAS. Alternatively, the complaint can be statutory, the final decision on which is taken by the Government (Ministry of Defence). Even a statutory complaint is processed through the Army Headquarters and carries the recommendations of the COAS before it goes to the ministry. The system of statutory complaint brings the bureaucrats in the decision making loop. Since the politicians generally lack continuity and do not have enough knowledge on the subject they invariably go by what the bureaucrats recommend. It quite often happens that while deciding on a statutory complaint the recommendations of the COAS are overturned by the ministry. This system opens the doors for the unhealthy practice of some officers bypassing the COAS and patronizing the bureaucrats. Apart from undermining the authority of the COAS this opens a vista for unscrupulous elements in the bureaucracy. While undoubtedly most bureaucrats are honest and principled, human nature being what it is, one cannot rule out unhealthy practices and as will figure later in this book even bribes come into play.

In their service, officers are rotated on regimental, staff and instructional assignments. The instructional assignments are given only to those officers who are recommended to be posted as instructors in their course reports written on them when they attend the various training courses during their service. The staff assignments are done at various headquarters such as Brigade, Divisional, Corps, Command and Army Headquarters. A common misperception among the uninformed is that only the best officers are posted to the Army Headquarters in New Delhi. The truth is just the opposite. The importance of a staff assignment is decided by the layers of supervision existing above that staff assignment in a particular headquarters. Lesser the layers of supervision, greater is the degree of independence for the staff to function and hence more important the staff assignment. For example, in the Army the smallest headquarters is a brigade headquarters. Therefore, the most competent officers would be posted to do a staff assignment in the brigade headquarters. The second best would go to the next level of hierarchy, i.e., a divisional headquarters, then to a Corps headquarters, still lesser merited to a Command headquarters and the lowest grade officers are normally posted to the Army Headquarters. This is based on the simple logic that in the Army Headquarters there are so many senior supervisory officers that an officer posted on the staff has a very slim chance of taking any independent action. There are, however, exceptions to this. Certain branches or directorates in the Army Headquarters dealing with important subjects, such as military operations and a few other chosen directorates have high calibre officers whose professionalism matches with those posted to a brigade or divisional headquarters. But in general the principle outlined here holds good.

The postings of officers in the Army are controlled entirely by the Military Secretary's Branch and individual officers have no control over when, where and in what assignment they are posted. In case an officer is chosen to be posted to an assignment which may have an adverse effect on his future career prospects, an 'adverse career certificate' is obtained from the officer before he is posted there. This absolves the system of any responsibility in case the officer's career is harmed as a result of such a posting.

2

Tenure as Military Attaché

I was the Military Attaché in France from December 1990 to August 1995. This was much longer than the normal tenure of three years. Some interested parties created an impression, that the longer tenure was at my behest or that I engineered it. The fact is that I was detained there against my wishes and to serve the interests of the Army. Reasons for my delayed repatriation are explained ensuingly.

I commanded a brigade in 1988-89 in the high altitude area of Sikkim, where we were in eyeball-to-eyeball contact with the Chinese. After I had finished approximately 18 months of command, I was called for an interview in the Army Headquarters. They had drawn a merit list of 20 Brigadiers from the Army for the post of Military Attaché in France. I was number one in the merit list. (I am mentioning this because it is relevant with respect to what will follow later). From these 20, after sifting, they short-listed six and called us for interview on 9 November 1989. Among these six, Brig JS Dhillon was from the 1961 batch and the remaining five of us were from the 1962 batch. The names of these five Brigadiers from the 1962 batch are given here in their order of merit:

(i) RS Kadyan

(ii) BS Malik

(iii) MM Belliappa

(iv) NC Vij

(v) MS Shergill

The interview was conducted by a high powered screening committee of four Lt Gens comprising the Vice Chief of Army Staff, the Deputy Chief of Army staff, the Military Secretary and the Director General of Military Intelligence. Since the committee only recommends the name, which is endorsed by the Army Chief and finally approved by the Ministry of Defence, it took some three months for the final decision to be taken.

On 14 February 1990 a signal was received from the Army Headquarters asking me to be attached to the Military Intelligence Directorate in Delhi with immediate effect for language training and necessary familiarization and formalities prior to proceeding to France. The signal mentioned that I was to move without relief and that the orders for the successor would be issued later. Keeping the brigade without a commander in the border area was not acceptable to the Corps. Besides, I was also the 'enemy commander' in the Divisional war game scheduled in end February, and my moving out at that stage would have upset the planned schedule. Army Headquarters therefore accepted the delay in my move on recommendation of the Corps and I finally reported in Delhi on 17 March 1990. This was only the first of many unfortunate delays in moving to and returning from Paris.

The post of a military attaché is a representational appointment. The host government has to give what in diplomatic parlance is called 'agreement,' which normally takes eight to ten weeks. In my case for some inexplicable reason, the 'agreement' papers were received only in end October 1990. The normal period of attachment with the Military Intelligence Directorate for an officer proceeding abroad to a non-English speaking country was four months. I, therefore, should have proceeded to France around middle of July 1990. However, due to the delay caused in the 'agreement' papers, I finally moved to Paris on 20 November 1990 and took up my assignment on 1 December 1990.

In December 1992 the Special Secretary (Security), who was part of a delegation visiting Paris, told me that the Military Wing in our Embassy in Paris was to be closed down and that a decision in this regard had already been taken. The Army authorities in Delhi had given me no information concerning this subject. When I contacted them, they confirmed the news and clarified that the closure was only temporary for a period of two years. It may be recalled that during that period our foreign exchange reserves were in a bad state and a concerted drive was apparently being undertaken to economise. The decision to cut out the Army and the Naval Wings in Paris was apparently part of this drive and was not based on any strategic considerations. A senior Defence Ministry functionary himself told me this while discussing the subject on a subsequent occasion. There are only seven posts of military attaches all over the world, which are held by officers of the rank of Brigadier; Colonels hold others. When I asked this functionary why we had selected Paris for closing down the Military Wing, his only comment was that our rentals in Paris were very high.

In April 1992 a Selection Board to select officers of our (1962) batch for promotion from Brig to the rank of Maj Gen was held. The results were conveyed to us in July 1992 where I was declared 'fit' for promotion. However, since I was holding the post tenable by a Brig, I could be promoted only on my return to India. Other officers who were junior to me started getting promotion to the rank of Maj Gen from September 1992 onwards. It needs to be mentioned that such delays are not uncommon, particularly for officers posted in our missions abroad. However, as per the existing system, whenever such officers get promoted subsequently, they regain their seniority and take their original slot in the ladder for further promotions.

In or around March 1993, I received an official communication from the Army Headquarters that we should close down and move back by 31 May 1993. However, the Ambassador on his own took up a case that since the academic session in Paris finished only in July, the move should be delayed till 31 July 1993. The Government accepted this and intimation was sent to us accordingly.

The Military Wing in Paris had files dating back to 1949. Since the closure was only for two years, these were to be catalogued, mothballed and put in storage. With only one clerk to assist, this was a Herculean task but we started our work in earnest. I also hired packers for moving household goods. I also booked our air seats back to India. In addition, the departure-related official functions commenced and we received a number of farewell dinners from friends. Since the Military Attaché in France was also concurrently accredited to Belgium, Holland and Luxembourg, there were a large number of official commitments that were gone through in those countries as well.

On 1 July 1993, Gen BC Joshi took over as the Army Chief. Gen Joshi apparently was not in favour of closing our Military Wing from Paris. Because, soon after he took over as the Army Chief – on 6 July 1993, to be precise – we received a message from the Army Headquarters that the date of closure was now postponed to 31 December 1993. The message carried reference of discussions Gen Joshi had had with the Defence Secretary, the Foreign Secretary and the Chairman of the Chiefs of Staff Committee. It seems this point carried priority with him and he got the earlier decision modified within a week of having taken over as the Army Chief.

I was then asked to prepare a detailed paper (called 'statement of case' in military parlance) justifying why we should continue retaining our Military Wing in Paris. *Inter alia,* I highlighted that it was against the interests of the country to close down one of the most important military outposts we had in the Western world. Numbering nearly 180 from various countries, Paris perhaps has the largest number of military attaches/representatives in the world. It provides an excellent contact point for sharing military-related information and to project our Government's views on various contemporary subjects. Besides, France is one of the leading countries as far as the military technology goes and it could be a very useful source of military equipment, more so after the break up of the Soviet Union. And of course, for projecting the professionalism and image of the fourth largest standing Army in the world, there is no better place than Paris. I also did some research to make a convincing case. Among other reasons I quoted figures of defence officers from different countries posted in their embassies in France. For example, Egypt had seven defence officers posted in Paris. Even Somalia, where there was practically no regular Army at the time, had a military attaché. Surely, our economy was not worse than these and many other countries similarly placed.

The statement of case was duly endorsed by our Ambassador.

In November 1993 there was a change of Ambassador and Mr Ranjit Sethi succeeded Mr Ranganathan. As I was to know later, Ranjit Sethi was a no-nonsense man. A polished diplomat in his fourth tenure as Ambassador, he was a very hard taskmaster and quite a terror for those who did not measure up to his standards. He spoke French fluently, though his main foreign language was Chinese. During his introductory round of the chancery (Embassy) building, when he came to my office, I told him that I was to close down and pack up on 31 December 1993. He was against closing down the Military Wing and said so emphatically. He wrote to the Foreign Secretary citing his own reasons against closure.

After I had sent the paper duly endorsed by the Ambassador, nothing more was heard from Delhi except hopeful assurances (from the Military Intelligence Directorate, which is the parent directorate for all military attaches) that we should succeed in retaining our presence in France. When December came and still there was no news, I began a direct telephone link with the Director General of Military Intelligence, Lt Gen SK Sharma. He kept telling me that the approval of the Government was expected any day and that I should plan accordingly. We, therefore, continued doing our normal work and did not close the office, which was essential if the documents were to be mothballed and stored. Lt Gen Sharma was a straightforward soldier who believed what perhaps the bureaucrats had indicated to him. However, around the third week of December or so, I started detecting a degree of frustration in his responses.

It was a difficult situation. If no orders came, I would become a *persona non grata* after 31 December. My household was in a semi-packed condition. My daughter had to be taken out of school. There were so many other administrative details that had to be buttoned up. In the last week of December 1993, therefore, I decided to sound a warning bell and share my dilemma with the Ambassador. Ranjit Sethi used his own channel to get a speedy decision. Finally, on 29 December, just two days prior to the date of closure, I received instructions from Delhi. Again, there was no reversal of the closing order. Only the date of closure was extended to 30 June 1994. I continued to live in a state of uncertainty.

As it invariably happens, I was required to forward another statement of case giving further justification why we should continue our military presence in Paris. This was done, and a comprehensive case duly endorsed by the Ambassador was forwarded. Then we waited. We had become a bit of a laughing stock with having announced twice that we would be leaving and then not doing so. Therefore, I wrote a letter to the Director General of Military Intelligence, Lt Gen SK Sharma on 12 April 1994, expressing my sentiments. A copy of the letter is reproduced below:

1. *I am writing this on the subject of the establishment of the Military Wing in this Mission. You are no doubt fully aware of the various statements of case and other documents forwarded by us recommending continuation of the Wing. The Ambassador too has thrown his full weight in support of our proposal and copies of various letters initiated by him in this connection have already been forwarded by us to the Military Intelligence Directorate.*
2. *As of now the Military wing here is to be retained only up to 30 Jun 1994. Earlier, we had been required to close down on 31 Jul 1993, postponed to 31 Dec 1993 and subsequently to the present date. This renewed lease of life has been coming at*

the last minute; in the latest case coming just two days before the deadline. Apart from causing uncertainty it creates innumerable administrative problems for all concerned, which, having been an Attaché yourself, you can well visualize. I request that a repetition of this be avoided by insisting that the Ministry take and convey their final decision at the earliest, not later than 10 May 1994. I do hope the decision is in favour of retention of the Wing, as we have been recommending.

3. I would like to reiterate that I have had my full tenure here and have no personal interest in any extension."

As would be seen, I had made it clear that I had no personal interest in staying any longer.

Sometime in May 1993 I received a telephonic message from Delhi informing me that the Government had finally given in to our persistence of continuing with our military presence in Paris.

In the last week of June 1994, the Vice Chief of Army staff, Lt Gen Surendra Nath visited Paris in connection with the Paris Air Show. He informed me that the process of selecting a successor for me had already begun and that they would surely position the man by Sep/Oct 1994 at the latest. He did not want the post to remain without an incumbent lest the Ministry should use this gap to prove their point that we can 'temporarily' make do without a Military Attaché. He wanted me to stay on till the arrival of the successor so that there was no gap between my departure and the arrival of my successor.

My daughter was studying in The International School of Paris and was to join Class XII in the final year of the school. That being a crucial class I did not want her to shift in the middle of the session. I, therefore, decided to repatriate her back to India immediately. She left Paris on 7 July 1994. Since the school admissions in India were already over, she had quite some difficulty in getting her admission in Class XII, more so because my wife and I were both still in France and my daughter was entirely on her own.

After the meeting with the Vice Chief of Army Staff in June 1994, nothing was heard from Delhi. When the month of October approached I started making enquiries again. Telephonically, I learnt that the process of selecting my successor in Paris had already started and that the new incumbent 'was about to come'.

On 18 October 1994, the Ministry of Defence sent a communication addressed to the Ambassador asking for my repatriation. Copy of the message is given below:

> *To*
>
> *Ambassador*
> *Embassy of India*
> *France (Paris)*
>
> *No.7 (15)/94/D (GS-III) (.) It has been decided to repatriate Brig R.S. Kadyan, Military Attaché in Paris as he has already overstayed his tenure (.) Ministry has already selected two officers to undergo language training in French before final selection for posting as Military Attaché (.) Till the arrival of the MA (designate) work of the Military Wing could be attended to by the Air Attaché or any other officer to be detailed by the HOM (.) Request early repatriation of Brig Kadyan (.)*

The above communication was signed by the Deputy Secretary and was addressed to the Ambassador. What was strange about the Defence Ministry's communication was that the Army was not aware of it nor was a copy endorsed to anyone in the Army Headquarters. When I spoke to the new Director General of Military Intelligence, Lt General JS Dhillon, he himself was surprised. He even checked with the Military Secretary and confirmed that the latter too was unaware of the message.

On receipt of the above message I pleaded with the Ambassador that I should be allowed to go back. I also pleaded that it might harm my career interests. However, since there was no mention of any adverse effect on my career in the Ministry's message, he refused to accept this plea and did not want a situation where there would be no Military Attaché in Paris. He accordingly sent a reply to the Ministry expressing these views and urging haste in the selection of the successor. A copy of his reply is reproduced herewith:

> *From:* *Indemassy Paris*
> *To:* *Ministry of Defence New Delhi*
> *RPT:* *Foreign New Delhi (for JS (W))*
>
> *Secretary (Defence)*
>
> *Nambiar from Ranjit Sethi*
>
> *Our conversation regarding Military Attaché Kadyan. As discussed, I believe there should be no gap between incumbents. I would thus request that the process of selecting and sending Brig. Kadyan's successor be expedited. With reference to Deputy Secretary Goyal's message of 18/10, I would be grateful if Brig. Kadyan is not disturbed for the moment and can remain till the arrival of his successor.*

I was not privy to the telephone conversation between the Ambassador and the Defence Secretary, Mr. Nambiar.

I was thus caught in a somewhat helpless situation, not at all of my own making. Our daughter was in Delhi. My wife continued to remain worried about her. We remained in a semi-packed state of perpetual uncertainty.

No response was received from the Ministry of Defence to the Ambassador's communication. About my successor, I continued to receive the 'about to come' assurance from the Army.

In December 1994, a Defence delegation visited Holland. Since I was also covering that country I joined the delegation. Mr RD Singh, a Joint Secretary in the Ministry of Defence (Finance), was part of this delegation. He told me of the government's decision to abolish the post of Military Attaché in Paris. I informed him that the government decision had since been reversed. He gave a new angle to it. He explained that the order to abolish the post was signed by the Defence Minister himself. The order reversing that decision was signed by the Minister of State for Defence. According to Mr Singh this was not accepted by the financial experts and in their view the post stayed abolished and I was there only on extension.

On returning to Paris I asked the Military Intelligence Directorate about what Mr Singh had stated. They confirmed that it was indeed correct and that they had already initiated action to get the signatures of the Defence Minister. The Prime Minister himself was handling the defence portfolio at that time. This technicality was a new impediment in the way of my repatriation and seemed to bring the situation back to square one.

I was thereafter in almost daily contact with the Army authorities in Delhi to check the progress. In early March 1995 they finally told me that the Prime Minister (as Defence Minister) had signed the order rescinding the earlier order and that the post of Military Attaché would continue in Paris. The Army had finally won its case. Since the highest executive authority had already signed the order there seemed no possibility now of anyone else sabotaging the issue.

By now I had spent four years and three months in Paris and my repatriation was long overdue. Many officers junior to me had already been promoted to the rank of Maj Gen; some had even finished commanding Divisions. Apprehending that the delay might adversely affect my future promotion to Lt Gen, on 11 March 1995 I wrote to the then Director General of Military Intelligence, Lt Gen Padmanabhan, with a request that I be recalled without relief. Copy of the letter is given below:

1. *As I have learnt telephonically, the Government of India has finally agreed to the continuation of the Military Wing in Paris.*
2. *I understand my successor's case is now being further progressed in New Delhi. Once every formality is completed, his agreement papers will be forwarded by the Ministry of External Affairs to the Embassy here. These will then be progressed with the French Government. The French authorities normally take two months to clear the papers. (With their preoccupation with the French Presidential elections scheduled on 23 Apr and 07 May 95, it is apprehended that they may take even longer.) My successor can plan his move only after his agreement papers have been finally cleared by the French Government. In the normal course, therefore, he is unlikely to reach here earlier than about 10 weeks after receipt of his agreement papers from our Ministry of External Affairs.*
3. *I have completed over four years in Paris and have thus stayed well beyond the normal tenure. While the*

case for the future of the Wing was in progress, I was not posted back as it was feared that the resulting gap in the Military Attaché's post could weaken our recommendations and could even result in our proposal being scuttled altogether. With the case having been finally cleared by the Prime Minister's Office, that danger has now passed.

4. *In view of the above, I request that my posting back to India may kindly be arranged without waiting for the relief.*

The Military Intelligence Directorate responded to the above request vide their fax dated 30 March 1995. It read:-

Reference your DO letter No 13153/RSK/DO/95 dated 11 Mar 95 (.) confirm if approval of HOM has been taken for repatriation without relief.

I had actually not consulted the Head of the Mission (HOM)/Ambassador before writing to the Director General of Military Intelligence on 11 March 1995. I now put a note on file and went up to him. I again pleaded with him that it was a question of my career and that any further delay would be detrimental to my career interests. By now he knew that the Prime Minister had approved continuation of the Military Wing and that it would not be possible now to discontinue the post. He therefore agreed though reluctantly. I sent the following fax to the Military Intelligence Directorate on 3 April 1995.

For DDG MI (FD) (.) Reference your fax A/87002/O/MI/FD (OA) Mar 30 (.) The Ambassador has approved my repatriation without relief (.) His remarks on the file are reproduced below (.) Quote (.) I have no objection to Brig Kadyan's repatriation without relief if it is unavoidable in view of his career interests. However, since the Military Wing does not have a

Deputy, it is advisable that the gap between the two incumbents is kept to the minimum (.) Unquote.

My posting was finally issued on 22 June 1995. I was required to take up my post as Inspector General Assam Rifles (North) in Nagaland in the rank of Maj Gen on 1 August 1995. I accordingly booked my passage back to India for 20 July 1995.

Subsequently, the posting order of my successor, Brig Ashok Hukku, was received in the first week of July 1995. He was required to report to Paris on 6 August 1995. The Ambassador again called me and pointed out that since the Army has delayed my move for so long, it makes no sense that I go away just two weeks prior to arrival of my successor. This way I would not be able to introduce him to the French Army authorities, to representatives of the French defence industry and other friendly 'contacts' which is essential for the post. He wanted me to hand over and then move. He remained firm despite my requests to the contrary and telephoned the Army Chief on the subject. The latter agreed and the Ambassador thanked him vide his letter dated 7 July 1995. It read:

I would like to thank you for agreeing so readily to the slight adjustment that I requested in the move from Paris of Brig Raj Kadyan.

As I mentioned, my request directly to you was a sign of the importance that I attach to some of the tasks Brig Kadyan has undertaken as Military Attaché.

I believe that I should emphasize that the initiative for the delay in his departure was purely mine; in no way did the officer seek it. Indeed he has been ready to move from Paris for a long time, having repatriated his daughter in July last year in preparation for his move. The extended stay of Brig Kadyan has been entirely due to his own move being linked to the fate of his post in Paris. As you might know, the abolition of the post, which was intended at the time I arrived in Paris, was unacceptable to me.

You will allow me to add that I have found Brig Kadyan an outstanding officer and a valuable asset to this Mission at all times.

When a Military Attaché takes up his post, he is totally new not only to the host country and the people but also to the job. It requires time for him to get to 'know the ropes'. Keeping this in mind, a period of 10 days overlap is given as time for handing/taking over between the old and the new incumbent. Since I was eager to come back early, the Ambassador permitted it to be reduced to seven days. Since Brig Hukku was reaching Paris on 6 August, I booked my return passage for 13 August 1995.

Ambassador Ranjit Sethi attached a lot of importance to the tasks undertaken by the Military Attaché. He also relied on the incumbent for advice on all defence matters. This is rightly so because a Brig being posted as military attaché usually carries with him over thirty years of experience in uniform in varied assignments and in a highly competitive environment. However, my experience shows that Ranjit Sethi was an exception in this regard. In many missions the military attaché lives a quiet life with hardly any recognition for his work. In keeping with this perception of his, Ambassador Ranjit Sethi planned to host a Reception on 9 August 1995 at his residence. I was asked to prepare the guest list so that I could introduce Hukku to all the people he would be working with during his tenure. This was a rare honour accorded to the post of Military Attaché by the Ambassador.

Unfortunately, Hukku (or someone in his family) fell sick and postponed his departure from India from 6 to 9 August. This would have meant his driving straight from the airport to the Reception. On my request the Ambassador agreed to let my departure on 13 August remain unchanged.

On 9 August we received another message that Hukku would now be arriving on 11 August. The Reception had to be held without him. The Ambassador now wanted me to postpone my departure. I assured him that I would work incessantly during day and night to put Hukku in full picture and that I should still leave on the 13th. Of course I had to concede that it would not be possible for me to take him around to meet all our contacts, more so it being a weekend. The Ambassador must have been cheesed off with my eagerness to depart because he finally agreed.

My bad luck did not end there. On 11 August we received another message from Delhi informing us that Brig Hukku would now be arriving on 13 August. This time the Ambassador did not get involved in any discussion. He called me to his office and simply handed me a note. Copy of it is reproduced below:

> *MA has been told to stay on for a smooth transition with his successor. However there has been some delay in the arrival of Brig Hukku. I regret that he was not present for the Reception on August 9. He was supposed to arrive on August 6, and we had expedited his agreement through the French Office; the date was later postponed first to August 9 and then August 11. This would have left hardly any time for handing over. I had suggested to MA that he postpone his departure. However, MA found this difficult and gave every assurance that he would provide the maximum briefings in the time available. I had agreed reluctantly.*

Now we have just heard that Brig Hukku will not arrive till August 13, also the day of Brig Kadyan's planned departure.

This would leave no time at all, rather than little time, for handing over.

In the circumstances, I am constrained to direct that Brig Kadyan postpone his departure so that there is an overlap of at least one week, if the normal ten days is not possible. If there is no overlap at all, our efforts to ensure smooth and efficient handing over will be defeated, out of concern for just a few days delay in the move of Brig Kadyan.

MA may inform Army Headquarters accordingly, if necessary send a copy of this note.

(Ranjit Sethi)
Ambassador
11.8.1995

I faxed the note immediately to the Director General of Military Intelligence. I did see the Ambassador's point. Leaving by the same flight by which my successor was arriving from Delhi, would make a mockery of his earlier request to the Army Chief to accept slight delay in my departure to permit proper handing/taking over. Actually the Ambassador had been more than reasonable.

I finally arrived in Delhi on 20 August 1995, after a total stay of 4 years and 9 months abroad, though I was perpetually on a short notice after I had completed two years of tenure. Starting from the middle of 1993, our household had remained in a semi-packed state. We had also sent our daughter back to India more than 13 months ahead of us. If we had the slightest inclination that we would remain there so long, she could have completed her Baccalaureate from the International School of Paris, one of the best schools in the world. The delay started right from the time I was to leave Sikkim for attachment with the Army Headquarters in February 1990. By the inability of Delhi mandarins to resolve a simple matter like continuation or otherwise of the military wing in Paris, the delay kept snowballing. However, I was confident that since I was not at all responsible for the extended tenure, the Army would protect my career interests. The military attaches, especially in the Brigadier's rank, are invariably behind their peer group for their promotion by the time they return from their foreign posting. The Army always protects their career interests and they catch up.

I have given the foregoing details only to inform the reader that the extended stay in Paris was not in any way on my account. The conclusive proof of it came from the Army Chief himself. When on a later date I filed a statutory complaint seeking government waiver to the requirement of commanding a Corps for minimum one year, the then Army Chief, Gen VP Malik, while recommending my case on 6 January 1998 had this to say, ... *On detailed examination I find that delay caused was due to circumstances well beyond the control of the Gen Offr and were primarily due to administrative constraints of the organization.*

3

The Nagaland Tenure

On return to India in August 1995, I was to take over the assignment of Inspector General Assam Rifles in Nagaland in the rank of Maj Gen. In that capacity I would be the overall operational commander of all the forces deployed in Nagaland. I received the news with mixed feelings. On the positive side was the fact that I had served in Nagaland twice earlier, once as a company commander in the rank of Maj in 1970-71, and second time as a battalion commander in the rank of Lt Col from 1978 to 1980. I had made many friends there with whom I had been in regular contact - in fact some Naga friends had requested me to be the local guardian of their children studying in Delhi. I was familiar with the genesis and the nature of the insurgency problem. The earlier assignments had given me an opportunity to tour the State extensively and I knew the terrain, the tribal set up, and had a good understanding of the psyche of a Naga. These would certainly be of advantage in tackling the problem and in directing counter-insurgency operations. Besides, with a heterogeneous force of nearly 35000 officers and men from the Army, the Assam Rifles, the BSF and the

Rashtriya Rifles, I would be commanding a force almost double the size of a normal Division. The insurgency was alive and active and therefore, I would be having a tough and a challenging assignment that should be the dream of any soldier.

However, there was a downside. The then Corps Commander was due for a change. The next incumbent, who would be a new promotee, had to be a 1962 batch officer. Since I was the seniormost Maj Gen of the 1962 batch, such an officer would be junior to me. This could lead to awkward situations as the Corps Commander who would be reporting on me, would also see me as a competitor for future promotions. I, therefore, decided to seek an interview with the Military Secretary and put forward my apprehensions. Accordingly, before leaving Paris, I wrote a letter to the Military Secretary on 14 August 1995, which is reproduced below:

1. *I have the honour to state that I will be passing through New Delhi next week, on my way to Nagaland. I request that I may please be granted an interview with the Military Secretary on 24 or 25 Aug 95, as convenient. My contact in New Delhi will be the office of the DDG MI (FD), telephone ...*
2. *During the interview I wish to be apprised of the steps being taken so that the inordinately long delay in my promotion to the rank of Maj Gen, caused solely in the interests of the Service and for no fault of mine, does not have any adverse effect on my long-term career prospects. In particular I want to request that:*
   (a) *The Military Secretary's Branch take all legitimate proactive steps to cut down the period before I am made eligible for consideration for promotion to the rank of Lt Gen. The steps I have in mind*

are special confidential reports, accelerated screening by the promotion board and whatever else permissible under the rules of the Military Secretary's Branch.

(b) In the meantime I am not made to serve under an officer who would have been my junior, but for the delay in my promotion to the rank of Maj Gen. Such a situation, apart from causing embarrassment, may also lead to competing career interests obscuring objectivity in reporting. I will happily and willingly accept a posting anywhere in the country, as also frequent transfers, if necessary for this purpose.

3. I am presently out of touch with rules and practices governing such interviews. Consequently, I am writing this with considerable apprehension, lest it be misunderstood that I am trying to manage my own career, instead of letting the Military Secretary do it. I am sure the Military Secretary's Branch, being well aware of the inordinate delay in my promotion must already be planning and taking all necessary steps – including the points mentioned in Paragraph 2 above – to make sure that my long term career interests are protected. However, since this is causing me anxiety and since I will be in New Delhi during the period, I thought I meet the Military Secretary and obtain reassurance right from the appropriate authority himself. In fact that will enable me to get this nagging thought out of my mind and focus my entire energy on the task that lies ahead of me. I hope my request will be seen in that light.

The interview took place on 25 August 1995, with the Military Secretary, Lt Gen Ravi Eipe and basically focused on two issues. First was related to my delayed repatriation and promotion to the rank of Maj Gen and what corrective steps would be taken to safeguard my future career interests. During the interview, this issue did not take much time. The Military Secretary stated that there was already a precedent of Lt Gen SK Sharma who similarly returned late from Germany. In his case he was made to command a Division (a criteria appointment mandatory for consideration for promotion to the next rank of Lt Gen) for the minimum required time and was made eligible for consideration for promotion to the rank of Lt Gen. (At the time of the interview, Lt Gen SK Sharma was already an Army Commander). He said he saw no reason why a different set of rules should be applied in my case. It needs to be clarified that the interview had no relation to my promotion to the rank of Lt Gen, which was premature at that stage since I was only just getting my promotion to the rank of Maj Gen. It was only concerning my eligibility for consideration for that promotion (to Lt Gen) at a later date, for which eligibility, a criteria assignment in the rank of Maj Gen was essential. (Inspector General Assam Rifles is a criteria appointment).

The second issue of being placed under a junior proved more tricky. The Military Secretary gave his views that such situations were not without precedent. He quoted an example of a similar situation where Lt Gen SK Sharma had commanded a Division when his junior VP Malik was commanding the Corps of which Sharma's Division formed part and where everything had gone well. That of course was true but then not all such instances have ended happily. I quoted another example where it was public knowledge that things had not gone so smoothly.

The discussion on this issue took most of the time of the forty-minute interview. Finally, the Military Secretary told me that in October 1994, after we had suffered quite some casualties in Nagaland, the then Army Chief, Gen BC Joshi had visited our units there. He came back very unhappy and on return had handpicked me to be the next commander of our forces in Nagaland. This, according to him, was mainly based on my experience of two previous tenures in Nagaland, one tenure in Mizoram and two tenures as Commando instructor in the Infantry School. All these assignments had a focus on unconventional operations, which was the requirement in combating insurgency. Once the Army Chief had selected me, thereafter, since it is a Home Ministry post, as per the Military Secretary, it took nearly five months to get my name approved by that Ministry and that there was no way it could be changed.

That seemed to conclude the interview and as I left, the Military Secretary remarked that in our system if one showed results in an assignment, no one would be able to keep him down. That was reassuring but as things unfolded, my apprehensions as well as his prophecy both proved right.

I took up my assignment in Nagaland on 3 September 1995. I earnestly applied myself to the problem of insurgency. The insurgents seldom face the security forces and instead engage only in hit and run tactics. Therefore, the combat part in insurgency scenario is basically confined to small sub units of the size of a company and below. The senior commanders can at best provide intelligence, concepts, ideas, motivation and a congenial environment where the unit commanders can operate without fear of making mistakes. Counter-insurgency operations are very difficult for troops traditionally trained and conditioned to conduct conventional operations where the adversary is clearly defined and identifiable. Therefore, mistakes are inevitable in conducting operations against insurgents who operate as and among civil population. I sent a clear signal down the line of command that for genuine mistakes committed in the line of performance of duties, no one would be punished or penalized.

The other role that senior commanders have to perform in these operations is management of the environment. In areas where insurgents wield influence, troops have to operate in a hostile environment. The press, the NGOs, local leaders and other opinion moulders all normally display an anti-security forces stance, most out of compulsion due to the fear of insurgents and a few, out of conviction. It was my effort to create a sense of security and an environment where the locals develop a genuine belief that the security forces are there to protect them and not to harass them.

I was operationally in charge of the whole of the State of Nagaland. I had a large force of nearly 25 battalions under my operational command. It did not take me long to get into picture as I already knew the terrain and the people and had wide contacts including with those members of the underground Army of the erstwhile Revolutionary Government of Nagaland that had surrendered and had been formed into BSF battalions. I had a civil telephone installed in my residence and gave it wide publicity through the press. I frequently got calls from all and sundry on various relevant and irrelevant subjects. Gradually this became a good source of intelligence and I started getting information about the locations, movements and plans of the insurgents. I also increased my contacts with the locals by joining them on various occasions connected with local traditions. We kept an open house and got many Nagas visiting us. I maintained very cordial relations with the politicians, the bureaucrats, other government functionaries, public leaders and common people.

In addition, I visited all the brigade and sector headquarters and units deployed in various parts of Nagaland.

I held operational discussions with officers of all ranks and met junior ranks. I was able to share my personal experiences of having commanded a company and later a battalion in that scenario. I also explained the warrior qualities and a straightforward character of a Naga. These were normal actions that any commander in my place would have taken.

While concentrating on the operational side, I also gave equal importance to winning the hearts and minds of the local people. We undertook a large number of humanitarian projects. These included construction of roads and playfields in remote areas, construction of school buildings, bus shelters, public toilets and community halls, holding of medical camps to provide free treatment and medicines, conducting training capsules to impart marketable skills to the rural people and various other similar schemes. I also frequently addressed the local people through the print and electronic media reminding them of the futility of continuing with the armed insurgency.

Our efforts began to show results. Lt Gen RN Batra, the outgoing Army Commander Eastern Command, wrote me a DO letter on the eve of his retirement on 29 February, 1996. It read:

1. *At the outset I am sorry, I could not attend the function you had planned during the middle of this month. I was looking forward to this event as one would have had yet another opportunity to see the impact of all that you have been doing in your area of responsibility for the last few months.*

2. *I take this opportunity to bid farewell and compliment you for the splendid manner in which you have been carrying out the most difficult task in a truly challenging environment. In a short span of time, with your refreshing indep of thought and dynamism, you have given a new thrust to the ops in Nagaland*

3. *I have no doubt with your deep involvement and spirited approach, you will continue to mount pressure on the UGs and bring them to the negotiating table soon. Here is wishing you Godspeed in all your endeavours. May your efforts bring glory to the Fmn and the Army in the years ahead.*

Troops in Nagaland performed well. During my two years of command, the units had conducted many successful operations. We also apprehended as many as six 'ministers' of the underground set-up. This was a major setback to their movement. That in the entire area of responsibility of the Corps, which included Nagaland, Manipur, Tripura and parts of Assam, a distinct improvement in the situation took place only in Nagaland, is a matter of historical record.

By early 1997, there were clear indications that the underground elements were prepared to negotiate with the Central government. Finally, the ceasefire came into effect on 1 August 1997. It was mainly as a result of our successful operations that one of the two main underground factions – Nationalist Socialist Council of Nagaland (Issac / Muivah Group) – accepted the ceasefire. This was the first time after 1975 that the underground factions accepted a ceasefire. This ceasefire is still lasting, and I do sincerely hope and pray that it leads to a permanent solution to the long-standing problem that has caused much misery and suffering to the Nagas and hampered developmental work.

On personal front what I had apprehended actually happened. My Corps Commander changed and Lt Gen SS Grewal took over as Corps Commander in October 1995. Grewal and I were from the same course (29th Course commissioned in June 1962) from the Indian Military Academy and he had passed out 111 places below me in the overall order of merit. There was only one more officer from our course who became a Corps Commander on 1 March 1996. He was Lt Gen HRS Kalkat. Kalkat was senior to Grewal but was junior to me by 40 numbers. He was promoted after Grewal (his junior) because Kalkat had been found unfit for promotion to the rank of Lt Gen in his first chance. He got this promotion through the route of a statutory complaint to the Ministry of Defence and was thus promoted later, though on promotion he regained his original slot above Grewal.

Since the appointment of an Army Commander is always made on the principle of seniority, fitness and (minimum two years) residual service, it was easy to calculate that from our course there would be only one officer who would become an Army Commander in the vacancy occurring on 1 March 1998. If I got promoted to the rank of Lt Gen, I would take over a Corps and being the seniormost, would then become an Army Commander. In case somehow my promotion to Lt Gen could be derailed, Grewal's friend Kalkat would get the post of Army Commander. And if something were to happen to Kalkat as well, Grewal would get it. A worse conflict of interests, as far as I was concerned, was difficult to imagine. But I remembered the words of the Military Secretary that if I showed results, no one would be able to able to keep me down.

Grewal was an infantry officer who had earlier been found unfit for promotion from Brig to Maj Gen and had subsequently attained that promotion through a complaint. We had known each other since our cadet days in the academy and had cordial relations throughout. Even in Nagaland we had no operational or work-related differences. However, it became obvious that he wanted to help Kalkat, and the only way to do so was to put me out of reckoning. That is precisely what Grewal tried to do.

It is a common practice that officers and men who have performed well in operational assignments are recommended for awards. Many were given awards on the Republic Day 1997. These included men and commanders at all levels that were operating below me as well as the Corps Commander. From bottom to top, the only one left out in hierarchy was me. In my case, as per procedure, the recommendation/citation for award had to be initiated by the Initiating Officer (IO) i.e. the Corps Commander, Lt Gen Grewal. As I learnt later, apparently having waited, the Army Commander himself initiated my citation the next year and I was awarded an Ati Vishist Sewa Medal (AVSM) on 26 January 1998, six months after I had moved out of that area. This must have been one of the rare cases in the Army when the recommendation was initiated by the RO instead of the IO. I need to mention here that no one has a right to demand an award and I was quite reconciled to the fact of not getting it. However, if I was found deserving and if an award had to be given to me, it would have carried greater significance and would have been more satisfying if it were given on 26 January 1997 along with others.

It is not that Grewal was generally tight-fisted in the matter of sending recommendations for awards. While denying me the award, he recommended Maj Gen NS Gill who was commanding the neighbouring Division in Manipur for AVSM. However, the award did not come through, probably because others in the chain of command did not support it.

Finally, Grewal tried to put me down in a very cleverly worded confidential report that seemed drafted by an expert. He wrote my report on 20 March 1998 that had been specially called for by the Army Headquarters in view of the Selection Board due in April 1998. From his side he wrote a report that would have rendered me unfit for promotion to Lt. Gen. However, as per established procedure, it was to be commented upon by the RO (Army Commander

Eastern Command) and the SRO (Chief of the Army Staff). Luckily, operational results achieved in Nagaland were well known to both. The Army Chief had paid a two-day visit to Nagaland for a first hand knowledge of the situation. Army Commander had of course been visiting often. Therefore, in his endorsement the RO must have commented that Grewal's report was biased, as being course-mates there was a clash of interests. On RO's recommendation the SRO apparently expunged from the IO's report whatever remarks were biased and were not compatible with my operational performance. The Army Chief, in the capacity as the SRO, has absolute powers to do so under the provision of Army Order, and the same has been done in other cases. Despite this provision as I learnt later, the Ministry of Defence raised an unprecedented query/objection in my case. Such was the 'interest' the bureaucracy was taking in the 'progression' of my career.

There was another important aspect related to the confidential report. Grewal wrote it on 20 March 1997 and I received an extract of it by post two days later. On the other hand, within hours of his writing it, a bureaucrat in the Ministry of Defence dealing with Army promotions, had learnt of its contents. An ACR is a confidential document and the contents are to be known only to the ratee and the reporting officer. Since I did not even see the report till two days after it was written, Grewal was the only other person who could have divulged its contents. Whether he himself conveyed the information directly to the bureaucrat, or whether he conveyed it through Kalkat, is anybody's guess.

I had already pointed out to the Military Secretary the undesireability of my being posted to serve under a batch-mate and an IMA junior. That was based on my apprehensions. I can now say with experience that even though Grewal was not able to harm my career or block my promotion to the rank of Lt Gen (just as the Military Secretary had mentioned during the interview that anyone who shows results cannot be kept down), it is incorrect of the system to create a situation where a senior is made to work under a junior who has competing career interests. It would be better for the organization as well as for the individuals, that such situations are avoided.

4

Promotion to Lt Gen

In October 1994, when I was still in Paris, officers of our (1962) batch were screened for promotion from Maj Gen to the rank of Lt Gen. Since I was still holding the rank of Brig and had not performed duties in the rank of Maj Gen, my case was deferred for consideration. This was communicated to me vide Army Headquarters letter No 30386/D/MS(X) dated 21 February 1995, which is reproduced below:

"Result of Special Selection Board Held on 21-22 Oct 94

1. *I am directed to inform you that you were considered by the above board for promotion to the rank of Lt Gen as a Fresh case of 1962 batch.*
2. *However, your case had to be 'Deferred' :*
   (a) because you have not done any criteria appointment.
   *(b) **************
3. *You will be considered in the next Selection Board and graded subject to the shortfall in 'Adequately Exercised' period as indicated in Para 2 above is either covered in the next CR or waived by the competent authority.*

I was again deferred in the selection boards held in April 1995, October 1995 and April 1996. Every time a similar communication citing absence/inadequacy of 'adequately exercised' period as the reason for deferment was sent to me by the MS Branch in the Army Headquarters. The reasons for deferment are always conveyed to the candidate officer.

The next selection board (fifth in my case) was scheduled to be held on 31 October 1996. As per procedure, a minimum of two reports are required in the rank of Maj Gen for an officer to be eligible for consideration for promotion to the rank of Lt Gen. My first report had been initiated on 1 July 1996 by Lt Gen Grewal as the IO. The Army Headquarters, under the provisions of Para 77(a) of Special Army Order number 3/S/1989, asked for a special report covering period upto 9 October 1996. Grewal having been away on leave during the period, I could not complete the minimum required 90 days service with him between I July and 9 October. Therefore, in accordance with Para 73 of the Special Army Order number 3/S/1989, and the procedure adopted in several other cases, the report was initiated by the RO (in this case the Eastern Army Commander), after obtaining sanction of the SRO (COAS).

The Selection Board assembled on 31 October 1996. Having taken over the appointment of Inspector General Assam Rifles on 3 September 1995, on this day I had completed 13 months and 28 days in the criteria appointment as Maj Gen and the Army Chief with the powers vested in him had waived off whatever shortfall there was in the Adequately Exercised period. As already brought out, the power to waive off a period exceeding three months is vested in the Chief of the Army Staff. The Army Chief had given similar waiver many times earlier to many other Maj Gens and there was nothing unusual in my case.

I was graded 'fit' for promotion by a unanimous verdict of the members of the Selection Board. The board proceedings were to be sent up to the Defence Ministry for obtaining approval of the Appointments Committee of the Cabinet, which includes the Prime Minister, the Home Minister and the Defence Minister.

In the last week of November 1996, I had come to Delhi to chair the Biennial Conference and to attend the Reunion of my Regiment, the Rajputana Rifles. Early morning on 26 November, Maj Gen GK Varma of my Regiment came to see me. He informed me that although the Selection Board had found me fit for promotion and had recommended my case accordingly, the Ministry of Defence was likely to change it to 'deferred' so as to accommodate another officer, Maj Gen BS Malik. It needs to be mentioned that BS Malik was from the same (June 1962) batch but was junior to me. The earlier Selection Board in April 1996 had found him 'unfit' for promotion to the rank of Lt Gen in April 1996. He was considered for the second time on 31 October 1996 where the Special Selection Board had again found him 'unfit' and had awarded grading 'Z'. As Maj Gen Malik was to retire from service on 30 November 1996, on attaining the age of 56 years, GK Varma told me that the Ministry was keen to promote him prior to his date of retirement and had changed his grading from 'Z' (unfit) to 'B' (fit). The position was that there was only one vacancy for a Lt Gen, and if both of us got approved, I would take that vacancy being senior and Malik would still retire on 30 November 1996, as a Maj Gen. Therefore, the Ministry had decided to 'defer' my case so that Malik could be adjusted. Varma suggested that we both go and meet the Defence Minister Mulayam Singh Yadav immediately in this regard.

It is my firm belief that if promotion of Maj Gen Malik was the only interest, the Ministry could have managed to accommodate both of us by creating an additional vacancy. However, the bureaucrats in the Ministry found this to be a good excuse to defer my promotion.

I had grown up imbibing the Army culture and had full faith in the Army authorities to take care of my legitimate career interests and I had never patronized any politician or a bureaucrat. I told Varma that I was confident the Army would stand by me and fight for my legitimate rights, and that I would not like to meet the Defence Minister. He apparently did not share my perception and told me categorically that while the decision of course was mine, I might regret it later. I stood by my decision.

The very next day, 27 November, I received a telephone call from a very senior Army officer dealing with my case in the Army Headquarters. He told me that they had tried their best to prevail upon the Ministry of Defence not to defer my case but had not succeeded. What he added thereafter really shocked me, and my entire faith in the ability of our hierarchy to protect interests of their officers stood shattered. He told me that if **I had any political connections I should use them.** I suddenly felt naked. The shield of the Army that I always imagined would guard me lay there in helpless shreds. All my confidence and my unbounded faith in the strength of the Army as an organization came crashing down. Here was the Army telling me to use political connections to get my legitimate due because they themselves were helpless. Nothing could be more disillusioning.

It became common knowledge that the Army made very strenuous efforts – the Army Chief reportedly even met the Prime Minister – to ensure that BS Malik's grading of 'Z' (unfit) awarded by the selection board was upheld. These efforts succeeded and on 29 November the Prime Minister as the head of Appointments Committee of the Cabinet, disagreeing with the Defence Minister, approved the grading 'Z' awarded to Maj Gen Malik. The Defence Ministry, however, played one up. On 29 November 1996, the day the ACC approved the 'Z' grading of Maj Gen Malik, they extended Malik's service by three months so that he did not have to retire on 30 November 1996. And before that period of extension expired, the Prime Minister was prevailed upon to change his own mind and change the grading of Maj Gen Malik from 'Z' (unfit) to 'B' (fit).

What efforts, if any, were made to prevail upon the ACC to uphold the award of grading 'B' (fit) to me by the Selection Board, is not known. The deferment of my case was confirmed by the ACC and the results were sent back to the Defence Ministry on 29 November 1996.

It needs to be pointed out that when the Selection Board considers a case and find that it does not have sufficient data in respect of a particular candidate officer to award a definite grading, it 'defers' his case, which in essence means that the case would be considered at a future date when sufficient data are available. This implies that only the Selection Board can decide the 'deferment' during consideration and the Defence Ministry or the ACC cannot award it. The ACC of course has the power to change the grading awarded by the Selection Board. This implies the change from 'fit' to 'unfit' and vice versa, as was done in Malik's case. In my case, in a departure from precedent and perhaps for the first time in the history of independent India, the Defence Ministry changed the grading 'fit' to the technical term 'deferred'. The Selection Board in fact had the required data to arrive at a definite conclusion and indeed had arrived at such a conclusion by a unanimous verdict. The Ministry could have changed the grading from 'fit' to 'unfit' (for which there were no grounds), but changing it to 'deferred' cannot be explained or understood. It may be useful to reproduce the notes exchanged between the Army Headquarters and the Ministry of Defence on the subject.

After the Selection Board was held on 31October 1996, the Army Headquarters sent the board proceedings to the Ministry of Defence for obtaining the approval of the ACC. The Ministry, on 8 November 1996, raised some queries, namely that a special CR had been called in my case, that I have not completed the 'adequately exercised' period and that the second report was written by the RO and not by the IO. The Military Secretary on 13 November 1996 replied to these queries as follows :

Maj Gen RS Kadyan (sl No. I)

1. *As per Para 77 (a) of the SAO 3/S/89, MS Branch can call for Special CR to assess an officer's fitness for promotion. Accordingly, Special CRs have been called for in the past in respect of officers of the entire batch or individual officers depending on merit of each case. We had called for the Special CRs of the officers of the entire 1962 batch of General Cadre upto 09/94 before Special Selection Board for this batch was initially held in Oct 94.*
2. *As regards Maj Gen RS Kadyan, his promotion to the rank of Maj Gen and placement in command was delayed in organizational interest. He was retained as MA France even after completion of the 3 years tenure because a protracted debate was on with the MEA on retention or otherwise of a Brig as MA in France and his juniors were promoted and placed in command before him. On repatriation from Paris, he was made IGAR (N) wef 03 Sep 95. As the officer*

was promoted late due to organizational constraints it is only fair that his career interests are protected by raising a Special CR for the period 01 Jul 96 to 09 Oct 96 under Para 77 (a) of SAO 3/S/89. The said Special CR was initiated by RO under the provisions of Para 73 of SAO 3/S/89 as Maj Gen Kadyan did not have 90 days physical service during that period under the IO, Lt Gen SS Grewal who was on leave from 12 Aug 96 to 07 Sep 96.

3. *Maj Gen Kadyan had completed 14 months against the prescribed 18 months in the criteria appointment as on 31 Oct 96 (date of holding Special Selection Board). The shortfall of 4 months in AE period has been waived by the Chief of the Army Staff as was done in the case of a number of other officers. Some of the General Cadre Officers who were given similar dispensation are:*

Name of the Officer	***Shortfall in AE period***
(a) GS Brar	*3 months 28 days*
(b) BN Kapur	*3 months 26 days*
(c) RK Sawhney	*3 months 29 days*
(d) Gurpreet Singh	*4 months*
(e) PK Puri	*3 months 4 days*
(f) SC Chopra	*3 months 5 days*

4. *Thus the officer has been considered and graded by Special Selection Board after following all the laid down procedure.*

The above Note or even the reasoning of the Army Headquarters, that all laid down procedure had been followed, was perhaps never sent by the Ministry of

Defence to the ACC when the board proceedings were forwarded. What was sent was a distorted and a biased version along with factual inaccuracies (read falsehoods). The Defence Secretary sent the following Note on 23 November 1996, to the ACC:

> *The Gen Officer has not completed the laid down "Adequately Exercised" period of 18 months. In fact the two reports which were considered for his promotion cover only a period of 11 months. Though in the past, some officers were given waiver upto 3 / 4 months on this count but the same was in order to provide opportunity to junior officers approved for promotion. This situation does not exist in his case. The waiver of 7 months in 'AE' in any case is not considered in order. The ground furnished by the Army HQrs that the officer had to overstay in France as Military Attache which led to delay in his promotion has also been examined in the Ministry but the same was not found satisfactory.*
>
> *In case of reports also, it has been noted that his second report covering period of 3 months was a special report initiated by RO directly as IO was not eligible to write the CR and was on leave. This was also carefully examined and it is considered that we must not give any impression that a special report was not initiated just to favour an officer.*
>
> *It is therefore recommended that the grading 'B'(C&S) (fit) be revised to 'D' (Deferred) in this case. He should be considered on completion of AE.*

It is relevant to note how the ACC was misled through falsehoods and factual twists. I took over my assignment as Maj Gen on 03 September 1995, and the Selection Board was held on 31 October 1996. As per orders and practice in vogue, the period is always calculated up to the date of assembly of the selection board. By no stretch of imagination can the period from 03 September 1995 to 31 October 1996 be calculated to be 11 months. But the bureaucrats made it so. They made it appear that while some others were given waiver for 3/4 months I was being given a waiver for 7 months and thus a special favour was being done to me. The actual waiver was only for 4 months as contended in the MS Note dated 13 November 1996. Normally, facts cannot be refuted, but the bureaucrats can do anything. **The secrecy of the notes they write gives them the smugness to state falsehoods without any fear.**

They also made it sound that a Special CR being called for in my case was some sort of an exception and was thus a favour was being done to me. To achieve this they concealed the fact that the Army Headquarters had earlier called for Special CRs for the entire 1962 batch, as well as the fact that Special CRs were being routinely called in many cases and a provision for this exists in the Special Army Order No 3/S/89. Ironically, even after this, and even in my own case, Special CRs were called for, covering period up to 10 March 1997 for the April 1997 Special Selection Board, and again covering period up to 31 January 1998 for consideration of my name for the Army Commander's post on 1 March 1998. The Ministry without any observation accepted both these Special CRs. It is difficult to avoid the inference that someone in the Ministry was especially interested in ensuring that I did not become Lt Gen in 1996.

Nor was initiation of the report by the RO instead of the IO an aberration of the provisions of the Special Order. If for some reason the IO cannot initiate the report, the RO can do it with permission of the SRO. This is provided for in the Special Army Order 3/S/1989 (Para73). Such cases are very common. For example even in my own case my CR on 1

June 1975 was written by the RO as the IO had been away on leave. In my service I had initiated many reports as RO as well as given permission as SRO for the ROs to initiate and all these were routinely accepted. There was no ground for the Ministry to raise observation on this count.

While singling me out for denial of the waiver, the Ministry tried to justify the grant of waiver to other officers on the ground that *'the same was in order to provide opportunity to junior officers approved for promotion'*. This is strange logic. First, waivers were granted not to officers 'approved for promotion' but before they were even considered for such approval. Secondly, if it was a valid reason, and not a mere excuse, then it raises many other questions. Why was the Ministry giving favoured treatment to junior officers at the cost of seniors? Was any other senior officer similarly deferred or was I the only one being singled out for discrimination? How can officers of a particular batch be subjected to two different kinds of treatment merely on account of their seniority? I was senior because I had passed out higher in the order of merit at the time of commissioning. If what the Ministry projected to the ACC is to be taken as correct, then by implication I was being penalized for being higher in merit vis-à-vis my batch mates. Not only this, the same Ministry took a different view in the case of Maj Gen BS Malik in whose case the Ministry had recommended a change of grading from 'unfit' to 'fit'. On 10 January 1997, the Defence Secretary sent a Note for the ACC. Para 8 of the Note reads:

> *Since many officers junior to Maj Gen BS Malik in 1962 batch have been promoted to the rank of Lt Gen and a recommendation was made to ACC to revise the grading to 'B' (fit) in his case, RM has also approved grant of extension of his service by 3 months, or till the declassification of the result of the special selection board held on 31-10-96, whichever is earlier.*

The above suggests that since many officers junior to Maj Gen BS Malik had already been promoted, he too should be promoted. In my case a contrary view has been taken. The adage 'you show me a person and I will show you a rule', seemed to apply in my case. Even a cursory analysis on these lines would show that the Defence Ministry's false and misleading projection of the case to the ACC was a clear attempt to support a pre-determined decision to deny me my promotion.

Coming to my extended tenure as MA in Paris, the Army Headquarters had all the documents on record where it was evident that the extension was not because of me but because of the organizational constraints. They also knew that I had even asked for repatriation without relief more than five months before I was actually moved back to India. What was it that was not found satisfactory by the Ministry? Did they expect me to leave Paris and come back to India on my own, without permission? There were no other documents and there was no correspondence other than what has been reproduced by me in earlier pages. It is not known and perhaps will never be known what was examined 'carefully' by them.

Finally the Defence Ministry had their way. The ACC deferred my promotion and the file came back to the Ministry on 29 November 1996. On the previous four occasions when I was 'deferred', absence/inadequacy of 'adequately excercised' period was always conveyed to me as a reason for the deferment. As an example let me reproduce Army Headquartes letter dated 30 July 1996 informing me of my deferment on an earlier occasion:

"Result of Special Selection Board Held on 24-25 Apr 96

1. *I am directed to inform you that you were considered by the above board for promotion to the rank of Lt Gen as a Fresh/Defer case of 1962 batch.*

2. *However, your case had to be 'Deferred':*
   - (a) ***********
   - (b) *On account of shortfall in the 'Adequately Excercised' period in the Command criteria appointments.*
3. *You will be considered in the next Selection Board and graded subject to the shortfall in 'Adequately Excercised' period as indicated in Para 2 above is either covered in the next CR or waived by the competent authority.*

This time no reasons were assigned. I was simply informed of the government decision vide MS Branch letter dated 10 March 1997, which read:

Result of Special Selection Board Held on 31 Oct 96

I am directed to inform you that you were considered by the above board for promotion to the rank of Lt Gen as a Fresh/Defer case of 1962 batch and have been awarded the grading 'Deferred' by the Govt.

This was a strange departure from the practice of informing an officer of the reasons why he is deferred. Obviously the Ministry had no valid grounds or reasons to convey to me. I wrote two applications – one on 8 March 1997, addressed to the Military Secretary and the other dated 28 April 1997, addressed to the Chief of the Army Staff requesting them to let me know the reasons why I was deferred. Till date I have not received a reply. The Army Chief must have been helpless in not knowing what to tell a serving General officer as to why he, as the Chief, was not able to protect his career interests after making him serve the interests of the organization.

It may be interesting to look at some of the notes exchanged between the MS Branch and the Ministry of

Defence after the results were declassified in February 1997, and my case was found to be finally 'deferred'. The MS Branch sent the following Note on 4 March 1997 :

> 1. *Min of Def is requested to intimate the reasons for altering the grading of Special Selection Board in the case of Maj Gen RS Kadyan, VSM to 'Deferred' before we intimate the result to the General Officer. This will enable us to meet the future requirement about the officer.*

On receipt of the above note the Under Secretary to the Ministry of Defence recorded the following note on 6 March 1997:

> 2. *Army HQrs have requested for reasons for altering the grading of Special Selection Board in respect of Maj Gen RS Kadyan, VSM from 'B' (fit) to 'deferred' before they intimate the result to the Gen Officer. They have also stated that the COAS had granted waiver of 4 months and 3 days in AE period in respect of the Gen Officer who had two command reports on record. They have further stated that the COAS had granted a similar waiver in cases of so many other officers in the past which was accepted by the Government.*

On the above note the Joint Secretary (G) in the Ministry of Defence had this to say on 13 March 1997:

> *We are not answerable to AHQ. We had raised observations on different officers seeking clarification. Encl 98 A refers. AHQ's replies were received and considered. Obviously those were not found satisfactory and hence the Board's proceedings were not agreed to in case of Maj Gen Kadyan. I do not find any reason to give any further response to AHQ.*

After my application dated 8 March 1997, seeking review of the change of grading to 'deferred' was received, the Army again approached the Ministry. The Under Secretary to the Ministry made the following comment on it on 31 March 1997:

> *Notes 139 and 140 will recall the case.*
>
> *Since no response was given to Army Hqrs. with reference to their note dated 4.3.97 (enclosure 135A), MS has requested to be apprised of the reasons for revising the grading in respect of Maj. Gen. R.S. Kadyan. A copy of an application received from Maj. Gen. Kadyan, has also been placed in the linked file. Maj. Gen. Kadyan in his application, has requested for review of the decision by the Government.*
>
> *As approved by the Defence Secretary in note 140 ante, no reply was considered necessary to Army HQrs. With reference to their note dated 4.3.97. As regards the application filed by Maj. Gen. Kadyan, we have taken a very conscientious decision, keeping in mind the rule position, to revise the grading. Therefore, no review in the Government decision is called for.*
>
> *It is for orders whether a reply need be sent to the Army Hqrs. or we may simply ask them to apprise the officer of the rule position.*

As transpired no reply was sent by the Ministry to the Army Headquarters. Perhaps it was not convenient for the bureaucrats to send a reply.

Subsequently, on receipt of my second application dated 28 April 1997, addressed to the Army Chief, the Army Headquarters took up the case again, belatedly, in August 1997. On this the Under Secretary to the Ministry of Defence prepared the following note on 3 September 1997 that went up to the Defence Secretary:

This is regarding approval of Special Selection Board proceedings held in Oct 96 in respect of General Cadre officers. Govt. had approved the Board proceedings subject to revision of grading from 'B' (Fit) to 'D' (Deferred) in respect of Maj Gen RS Kadyan and 'Z' (Unfit) to 'B' (Fit) in respect of Maj Gen BS Malik. MS Branch vide their note at encl. 135-A and note 3 in the linked file desired to know the reasons for revision of grading in respect of Maj Gen RS Kadyan. The matter was examined vide notes 136 to 140 ante and with the approval of Defence Secretary, it was decided that no formal reply be sent to Army HQrs and their attention be drawn to Para 2 (i) of ID Note No. 2438?MS/JS(G)/96, dated 8.11.96 under which observations were made on MS Branch in respect of certain cases including that of Maj Gen RS Kadyan.

Now after a gap of four months, MS Branch have again raised this issue vide note 5 in the linked file. They have stated that waiver of four months in a similar case of Maj Gen (now Lt Gen) Gurpreet Singh was earlier accepted by the Government and that more than adequate response was made to MOD ID Note dated 8.11.96, MOD reply vide note 4 on their linked file was considered inadequate. They have therefore requested that this aspect be examined again and suitable reasons be given so that a reply be given to the officer.

We have already examined this issue earlier and there are no justifiable reasons to reopen this case. The General officer has been considered in the April 97 Board and graded Fit for promotion. There is no need to send a reply to Army HQrs or to the officer.

In a democratic set up the Armed forces have to essentially function under civilian control. There is no dispute in that. However, one has to understand what is civilian control. It is the control by politically elected leaders. But as is seen in this case, (and there would be many other similar cases), in actual practice it amounts to bureaucratic control. The MOD bureaucrats overrule a decision made by the Chief of the Army Staff of the fourth largest Army in the world. The anomaly of the system can be better understood when one realizes that the Army Chief is senior to the highest MOD bureaucrat - the Defence Secretary - in the national Order of Precedence. What is even more frustrating is that while rejecting the waiver given by the Army Chief under his powers, the bureaucrats do not even consider it necessary to assign a reason or to explain why a Kadyan is singled out for rejecting a waiver while it was given to a Gurpreet Singh and to many others in the past. In fact they are so sure of (mis)using this self-acquired power that an officer of the Joint Secretary level can openly endorse on the file *'we are not answerable to Army Headquarters'*, that too in response to a legitimate query. The unfortunate fallout of this is that some unscrupulous senior Army officers tend to play to the tune of the bureaucracy, bypassing their Chief.

As would be seen from the above notes, **the political bosses, who are to exercise the civil control over the armed forces, are not even kept informed, leave aside being in the decision-making loop**.

The change of my grading from 'fit' to 'deferred' was not the only unusual action taken by the Ministry of Defence. A few other related actions clearly show that there was someone in the Ministry who was working hard to ensure that I do not get the Army Commander's post whenever my turn came. Since I did not have any direct contact with any one in the Ministry, I could not have had any personal animosity with anyone. It is obvious to me that the actions were directed towards helping someone else lower down in seniority.

The results, in which my deferment was approved by the ACC, came back to the Ministry of Defence on 29 November 1996. Under normal circumstances, and there being no apparent reason to withhold, these results should have been declassified immediately. But someone in the Ministry saw a danger in this. The next vacancy for an Lt Gen was to occur on 1 February 1997, on the retirement of Lt Gen KL D'Souza. If the results were immediately declared, there was every likelihood that the Army would convene another Special Selection Board in which I might be approved and then got promoted to take this vacancy. (Although the Special Selection Board normally convenes twice a year i.e. in April and October to coincide with the Army Commanders bi-annual conference, there have been several occasions when this Board has assembled at other times. For example, ad hoc Special Selection Boards were held in August 1993, November 1993, January 1994, July 1994, September 1995, December 1995, etc.) This would still give me enough time (of 13 months) after becoming a Lt Gen to take the Army Commander's post that was to fall vacant on 01 March 1998. Therefore, something had to be done to defeat this time frame. Apart from the unprecedented action of changing my grading of 'fit' to 'deferred', two other actions were taken. Firstly, the declassification of the Promotion results was delayed from 30 November 1996 to end February 1997 without any reason or logic except some vested interests. Since the results of the earlier selection board were not yet officially declared, the Army could not plan to convene another selection board.

There was yet another peculiarity of the board results. As already brought out, this time, unlike on previous occasions, the letter from the Army Headquarters did not give any reasons as to why I had been deferred.

The third action of the MOD was to amend the Government letter dated 20 October 1986, which deals with the appointment of Army Commander. This letter stipulates only two conditions of eligibility. Firstly, the officer should be fit in every respect for the appointment, and secondly, the officer should have two years of residual service left at the time of appointment. Now, after my Selection Board had already been held on 31 October 1996, and when the proceedings were still under process, the Ministry issued another letter on 18 November 1996. This letter made it a mandatory condition for an officer to command a Corps for at least one year before being eligible for the appointment of Army Commander. This letter was actually an amendment to the original letter dated 20 October 1986. Both the letters read as follows:

No18684/JS(P&W)/86
Government of India,
Ministry of Defence, New Delhi,
October 20,1986

To
The Chief of the Army Staff,
New Delhi.

Subject: Appointment of Army commanders/VCOAS – Criteria for Selection – Policy.

Sir,

I am directed to say that the President is pleased to lay down the following criteria for the appointment of the Army Commanders/VCOAS :-

(a) The officer should be fit in every respect for such appointment; and

(b) The officer should have a minimum of two years left before the retirement age from the date of appointment as Army Commander/VCOAS.

(c) This will be applicable w.e.f. 1.1.1988.

(d) As a one time exception, the pay but not the status of an Army Commander will be given to those General Officers, presently holding the rank of Lt. Gen. Who are otherwise found fit to hold the appointment but are not selected because of the revision in the criteria.

Yours faithfully,

(Dhirendra Singh)
Joint Secretary to the Government of India
Copy for information to:.......

The second letter No 19(24)/96/D(MS) dated 18 November 1996, amending the above letter read as under :

I am directed to refer to Government of India, Min of Def letter No 18684/JS(P&W)/86 dt 20th Oct 1986 and to request that the following clause (e) may be added at the end of the letter:

(e) The officer should have commanded a Corps for at least one year so as to become eligible for appointment as Army Commander/VCOAS. No waiver in this stipulation will be allowed without prior concurrence of the Government.

(A K Jain)
Joint Secretary to the Government of India

As would be seen the original letter dated 20 October 1986, was to take effect from 1 January 1988, that is, nearly fifteen months after it was issued. This is the normal practice whenever government orders laying down new stipulations that affect service conditions are issued. This practice ensures protection of career interests of those officers who are adversely affected by the issue of revised government stipulations. Significantly, the amendment to this letter issued on 18 November 1996, was made applicable from the very date of issue and no lead-time was given. The other peculiar aspect of this 18 November letter was that in the entire Army I was the only officer affected by it immediately as well as in the foreseeable future.

It is not difficult to see that the combined result of the three actions of Ministry of Defence, i.e. change of my grading from 'fit' to 'deferred', delay in declassification of Board results and laying down of a fresh condition of eligibility of one year command of a Corps was to put me out of reckoning for the appointment of an Army Commander. It seems obvious that someone in the Ministry was trying to either harm my interests, or was trying to promote the interests of someone else and I just happened to be in the way. The seniormost bureaucrat in the Ministry, i.e. the Defence Secretary, did nothing to correct the arbitrariness of the actions of his Ministry.

Promotion to Lt Gen

The next Selection Board was held on 10 April 1997. I was again declared 'fit' by a unanimous decision of the board. I thus had the unique 'honour' of being found fit for promotion to the rank of Lt Gen twice by the Selection Board. This time even the Ministry of Defence did not play around with the results and these were declassified on 08 July 1997. There was another development that took place during this period. One Maj Gen HS Bagga had gone to court against his non-promotion to the rank of Lt Gen. In July 1997 the Delhi High Court had upheld his plea and had stayed all promotions to the rank of Lt Gen till Bagga was promoted. This court order was an impingement on government's prerogative to carry out promotions of their employees. Government always challenges such orders in the Supreme Court. However, this time the order was not challenged. It could not have been a mere coincidence that I was mainly the officer adversely affected by the Delhi High Court order, and this was very much foreseen.

My posting order to be General Officer Commanding (GOC) 1 Corps was issued on 06 August 1997. I was to assume my new appointment on 23 August 1997. However, due to the stay order of the Delhi High Court on promotions (in Maj Gen Bagga's case), the posting order while giving me the appointment of GOC 1 Corps could not give me the rank of Lt Gen. The wording used in the posting order was *'to look after work of GOC 1 Corps'.* The Military Secretary during our meeting told me that this peculiar wording was only to avoid contempt of court. It did not in any way affect my performance of duties.

It needs to be pointed out that after joining as GOC of 1 Corps, I was the seniormost officer in the Corps, I occupied the Corps Commander's chair and exercised all the powers, performed all the duties and assumed all the responsibility of a Corps Commander, and there was no one else posted as Corps Commander of 1 Corps. The Appointments Committee of the Cabinet had approved my appointment as Corps Commander in July 1997, before the stay imposed by the Delhi High Court. I was without doubt in command of the Corps and was getting experience of that post. The only difference was that I was holding the rank of Maj Gen instead of Lt Gen. **But the experience of a post is related to a person and not to the badges of rank he wears on**

his shoulders. Besides, the Government order dated 18.11.1996 laying down the stipulation of minimum one year command of a Corps as eligibility for the post of Army Commander does not specify that this command has to be in the rank of Lt Gen only.

On the very day that Maj Gen Bagga was promoted and the court stay was lifted, I was promoted to the rank of Lt Gen on 24 September 1997, and I continued performing the same duties that I had been performing since 23 August 1997.

Whenever an important happening takes place in the Army, it is notified through the publication of what in military parlance are called Part II Orders. When I joined HQ 1 Corps on 23 August 1997, the Part II Order No 114 dated 25 August 1997 published by the Corps said, "TOS (taken on strength) from HQ IGAR (North) on permanent posting to carry out the duties of GOC 1 Corps". Again on my promotion to the rank of Lt Gen, Part II Order No 115 dated 25 September 1997 said, "Continues to hold the appointment of GOC 1 Corps wef 24 Sep 97 in the new rank".

Copies of these Part II orders were endorsed to many addressees, including five different branches of Army HQ. These were accepted by all, without any observation.

It would thus be seen that from 23 August to 23 September 1997 I was carrying out the duties of Corps Commander and was gaining experience of that post. I am stressing this point because it is relevant to what happened subsequently during hearings in the Supreme Court.

5

The Appointment of Army Commander

In the Indian Army till 1985 the seniormost Lt Gen found fit was appointed Army Commander irrespective of his residual service left prior to his retirement. Thus even if a Lt Gen had only a few months left before retiring, he was also appointed Army Commander. Realising that in order to do justice to the job the Army Commander should have a minimum tenure in that appointment, in 1985 it was laid down that the officer should have a minimum of one year of residual service. The very next year, by a Government order dated 20 October 1986, this residual service was increased to two years. This order has already been reproduced in the previous chapter. However, for ease of reference extract of it is once again reproduced below:

Subject: - Appointment of Army commanders/VCOAS – Criteria for Selection – Policy.

Sir,

I am directed to say that the President is pleased to lay down the following criteria for the appointment of the Army Commanders/VCOAS:

(a) *The officer should be fit in every respect for such appointment; and*

(b) *The officer should have a minimum of two years left before the retirement age from the date of appointment as Army Commander/VCOAS.*

(c) *This will be applicable w.e.f. 1.1.1988.*

(d) *As a one time exception, the pay but not the status of an Army Commander will be given to those General Officers, presently holding the rank of Lt. Gen. Who are otherwise found fit to hold the appointment but are not selected because of the revision in the criteria.*

To understand the true import and motive of this order, it is essential to know how a Lt Gen is appointed an Army Commander (also referred to as the General Officer Commanding-in-Chief, or GOC-in-C for short. The posts of GOC-in-C and Vice COAS are at par.) The only criteria are that the officer should be fit for the job and should have two years residual service left. Apart from his medical fitness he should also be professionally fit and competent. The sole yardstick for judging and recording the professional fitness is through the medium of ACR. Out of the available and eligible (in terms of two years residual service) Lt Generals, the scrutiny starts from the seniormost officer, and if he is found fit he is appointed. In case the seniormost is not found fit then only the next in seniority is considered. The criterion therefore is seniority-cum-fitness. The merit of an officer has already been established during the five selection boards that one has gone through to reach the rank of Lt Gen. Also, since Army Commander is only an appointment (in the same rank of Lt Gen) and not a promotion, the seniority-cum-fitness criterion is followed. Besides, the professional fitness has already been judged at the time of his consideration for the rank of Lt Gen, where all his record up to that stage has been scrutinised.

The only additional input after that is the ACR written on the officer in the rank of Lt Gen as Corps Commander. If in that report the answer to the two simple questions '*Do you consider him fit in every way to hold his present rank?*' and '*Do you consider him fit for promotion to the next rank/ appointment?*' is 'yes', the officer is considered fit to be appointed as Army Commander. There is no comparison between different eligible candidates. This is apparent also from the ACR form for a Lt Gen where there are no numerical grades that could permit comparison.

As would be seen this government letter dated 28 October 1986, has only two eligibility conditions given in sub clauses (a) and (b) i.e. fitness and residual service. This is also evident from use of the word 'and' at the end of sub clause (a) and a full stop at the end of Clause (b) Clauses (c) and (d) are not eligibility conditions and are only administrative in nature. This is how this letter has always been interpreted and implemented all along since its issue. This is how it continues to be implemented even today for all the appointments of Army Commander made after I was deprived of that post. The only exception that has ever been made was in my case.

To ensure fairness, the order, though issued on 20 October 1986, was made applicable some fifteen months later that is with effect from 1 January 1988. Besides, those immediately affected by it were given the pay of an Army Commander. This type of lead-time is invariably given whenever there is a change in government rulings. In the light of this one needs to examine the government order dated 18 November 1996.

The 18 November 1996 order was actually an amendment to the earlier government order dated 20 October 1986, in that it added a sub clause (e) at the end of the existing four sub clauses of the earlier letter. Whereas the main order was given fifteen months of lead-time, the amendment, for some inexplicable reason, was made to take effect from the very date of its issue. Secondly, it was well known that I was the only officer affected by it in the immediate as well as in the foreseeable future. May be just a coincidence, but the only gainer was Lt Gen HRS Kalkat.

However, the Government letter dated 18 November 1996, carried a provision for a waiver though only with the approval of the government.

The Statutory Complaint

Since the appointment of an Army Commander is always made based on the seniority-cum-fitness principle, it had been known by simple arithmetic calculation that being the seniormost Lt Gen I would be due for consideration for the appointment of Army Commander on 01 March 1998, on the retirement of Lt Gen Ravi Eipe, the then Eastern Army Commander. However, with the new stipulation of minimum command of a Corps for one year I would not be eligible, unless a waiver were asked for and granted by the government. Therefore, soon after being promoted to the rank of Lt Gen on 24 September 1997, I put up a statutory complaint on 5 October 1997, seeking such a waiver. Although it was a request for grant of a waiver, the procedure demands that it has to be obtained only through a 'complaint'. In fact the only channel open for an Army officer to communicate with the Central government is through the medium of a complaint.

The theme of my complaint was that since the delay in my taking over the command of the Corps was a direct result of my late repatriation from France, on which I had no control, a waiver was required. In this complaint I also touched upon the arbitrary action of the government in changing my grading of 'fit' to 'deferred' in the October 1996 selection board and requested redress. Since extract of the complaint was quoted in the Supreme Court judgment, it would be useful for me to reproduce the entire complaint (less the appendices mentioned therein as these already appear elsewhere):

Gist of the Complaint

1. I am an infantry officer of Jun 1962 batch. I am presently commanding 1 Corps. Based on my merit-cum-seniority, and subject to my being found fit in all other respects, I am eligible to become an Army Commander on 01 Mar 1998. However, certain recent decisions of the government may deny me my legitimate due. This complaint pertains to seeking review of/waiver from such government orders with a view to protecting my career interests.

Main Points of the Complaint

2. In Nov 1990, I was posted as Military Attaché in Paris. The normal tenure for as Military Attaché is three years, whereas I was kept in that appointment for over four years and eight months. Had I been posted out after my normal tenure of three years, I would have been promoted and taken over a division and subsequently a Corps well in time. Of course, I would have been delayed for promotion to the rank of Maj Gen some bit, but it would not have had any cascading effect on my future promotion. In fact, I believe that kind of delay is a norm with most Military Attaches, particularly of Brigadier's rank, and foreseeing this the Army Headquarters routinely obtain an 'adverse career certificate' from all of them before posting them abroad, which I too must have given. However, as mentioned earlier, it is not that normal tenure of three years, which could have done any damage to my long-term career prospects. But the extension of the tenure

by that additional period of over twenty months, over which I had no control and for which I was in no way responsible, now may do just that.

3. The delay in my reversion from Paris occurred as my appointment there got tied up with the bigger decision whether there should continue to be a Military Attaché and a Military Wing at our Embassy at Paris or not. In November 1992 the Ministry of Defence (MOD) decided to close the Military Wing in our Embassy at Paris. This decision was to take effect from 31 May 1993. The date of course, however, got changed four times. It appears that the reason for this change was the fact that the other two government agencies, namely the Army and the Embassy of India, Paris, were not fully with decision to close down the Military Wing. The Army represented that it is essential in the interest of Service to maintain the Military Attaché's post and the Military wing in Paris. The Embassy, while taking a similar stance, further insisted that there should be no break in the continuity of the presence of a Military Attaché in Paris and requested that my successor be posted at the earliest.

4. Finally, in May 1994 the MOD reversed its earlier decision to close down the Military Wing. In the eighteen months between November 1992 and May 1994, no action was apparently taken to select my relief.

5. I had already completed my three years tenure on 01 Dec 1993 and had no personal interest in seeking any further extension. I conveyed this to my immediate superior, the then Director General of Military Intelligence (DGMI) vide my letter No 305/01/MA dated 12 Apr 1994, copy of which is attached as Appendix 'A'.

6. Based on the MOD decision of May 1994, and expecting to be relieved soon, I split my family and repatriated my daughter to India in July 1994 as I did not want her to change schools in the middle of her crucial 12th grade. However, after that it took thirteen more months for my successor to reach Paris, which he did in Aug 1995. Keeping an 18-year-old girl away from parental care and guidance was a major concern for my wife during that period. However, this I suppose is a part of Army life.
7. In Oct 1994 the Ambassador received a telex message No 7(15)/94/D/(GS-III) (PC) dated 18 Oct 1994, (Copy attached as Appendix 'B') from the MOD asking for my repatriation without relief as I had already overstayed my tenure. I requested the Ambassador to allow me to return as requested by the MOD. However, he did not agree to there being a gap between my departure and arrival there of my successor. Accordingly, he sent a fax message on 19 Oct 1994 to the Defence Secretary. Copy of the fax is attached at Appendix 'C".
8. In Dec 1994, Mr. RD Singh, Joint Secretary (Finance), who met me during a delegation visit to Holland, informed me that the Finance had not accepted the reversal of the MOD decision and as per them (Finance) the establishment of the Military Wing in Paris stayed cut and that we were there only on extension. I rechecked this from the Military Intelligence (MI) Directorate and learnt that this was correct. I was informed that the matter was referred to the Prime Minister (who was also the Raksha Mantri) for final decision. From then I kept checking the progress with the MI Directorate regularly as I was anxious to return. As soon as I learnt (telephonically) that the Prime

Minister had finally approved the continuation of the Military Wing in Paris, I wrote to the DGMI to have me posted back without relief. Copy of this letter No 13153RSK/DO/95 dated 11 Mar 1995 is attached as Appendix 'D'.

9. My posting was finally issued and I was required to report to Army Headquarters on 26 Jul 1995. However, my successor's Agreement Papers had got delayed at the Delhi end (once they reached Paris on my request the Ambassador intervened with the French government to get their 'Agreement' faster than the normal time and in the first week of Jul 1995 it became known that he would reach Paris only on 06 Aug 1995. This would have created a gap of approximately a fortnight, which again was not acceptable to the Ambassador. He, therefore, telephoned the Chief of the Army Staff (COAS) and requested for a slight delay in my departure from Paris, which the latter agreed. In this connection copy of a fax message dated 07 Jul 1995 from the Ambassador to the COAS is placed at Appendix 'E' attached.

10. I made my air booking from Paris to Delhi on 13 Aug 95. Unfortunately my successor, Brig Hukku and his family came down with a viral fever in Delhi and could not fly to Paris on 06 Aug 1995, as planned. He had to postpone his move from 06 to 09 to 11 and finally to 13 Aug 1995. As a consequence my return to India also got postponed from 13 to 20 Aug 1995. In this connection a copy of Note from the Ambassador dated 11 Aug 1995 is enclosed as Appendix 'F'.

11. I finally arrived in India on 20 Aug 1995, after a tenure of over 4 years 8 months. However, I neither tried for any extension nor was I in any way responsible for it.

The extended tenure was entirely in the interest of Service. It is pertinent to mention that Shri Ranjit Sethi still continues to be our Ambassador in Paris. If required, the facts may be verified from him.

12. Undoubtedly, there were valid reasons necessitating the changes in the date of closure of Military Wing and final reversal of the decision. All the same it was natural for me to be concerned about their impact on my career prospects. Consequently I expressed them to the Military Secretary during an interview on 25 August 1995. I am attaching (as Appendix 'G') a copy of my request for the interview which is self-explanatory. During the interview I was happy to learn that the Army was already fully seized of my career situation and was no less keen to get it back on track and that I needed to focus solely on the tough job that lay ahead of me.

13. I was considered for promotion to the rank of Lt Gen by Special Selection Board in October 1994, April 1995, October 1995 and April 1996. I was deferred on all four occasions. On each occasion Army Headquarters conveyed the reason for such deferment to me, which was 'on account of shortfall in the 'Adequately Exercised' period in the command criteria appointments'.

14. I took over the appointment of IGAR (N) on 03 September 1995. I was again considered by the Special Selection Board held on 31 October 1996. In Mar 1997 Army Headquarters informed me that I had been awarded the grading 'deferred' by the government. This time no reasons were intimated to me for the deferment. I had earlier learnt through press reports (*Jan Satta*, New Delhi, 18 Jan 1997, copy attached as Appendix 'H') that I had been approved by the Army

but was deferred by the MOD. I could not understand the reasons for this action of the government. I had done adequate time in the command assignment and for any short fall in it the COAS had given a dispensation under the existing rules and based on precedence. Having taken over the appointment of IGAR (N) on 03 September 1995 I was considered by the Selection Board on 31 October 1996, on which day I had completed 13 months and 28 days in my command. There have been several cases in the past where officers with similar or even lesser period in the command criteria appointment have been considered by the board without any objection raised by the MOD. In fact, as known to me, mine is the first case where a dispensation allowed by the COAS has been vetoed by the MOD.

15. Since no reasons were intimated for the deferment, on 08 March 1997 I sent an application to the Military Secretary (copy attached as Appendix 'J') requesting for a review of the government decision. No reply has been received till date. Subsequently I sent another application No 13153/RSK/97 dared 28 April 1997 (copy attached as Appendix 'K'), addressed to the COAS again requesting for a review of the government decision. This application also has fetched no response till date.

16. I was put through the next Selection Board on 10 April 1997. In this Board I was finally approved and the results were intimated to me vide Army Headquarters letter No A/47050/Gen Cadre/MS(X) dated 08 July 1997. Even after that I was posted to take over the Corps only on 23 August 1997, a delay of over six weeks after declaration of results. Further, even though I started performing duties of GOC 1 Corps from 23

Aug 1997, I was not allowed even the local rank of Lt Gen till receipt of Army HQ Sig No 385327/97/MS(X) dated 23 September 1997.

17. As a result of my deferment in the October 1996 Selection Board and subsequent delay in my promotion, the following officers who are junior to me were promoted during the interim period:

    (a) Lt Gen BS Malik

    (b) Lt Gen Krishan Pal. (Still in local rank)

    (c) Lt Gen SC Chopra

18. If, instead of being deferred I had been approved in the October 1996 Selection Board, then, being the seniormost I was likely to have taken over a Corps immediately on declaration of the board results as the following vacancies were in existence :

    (a) DG NCC from 01 October 1996

    (b) DCOAS from 01 January 1997

19. Simultaneously with my deferment in October 1996 Selection Board the MOD issued letter No 19/(24)/96/ D(MS) dated 18 November 1996 laying down that henceforth an officer, to become eligible to be an Army Commander, should have commanded a Corps for at least one year. There have been many officers in the past (such as Late Lt Gen Jameel Mahmood, Lt Gen AK Gautam, Lt Gen SK Sharma) that commanded a Corps for less than one year and became Army Commanders. This is the first time that the government has stipulated this condition of minimum one-year command of a Corps. What is more, at the time of issue of the 18 Nov 1996 letter, as also of now, this order affects only one officer in the whole Army, and that is me. It is also pertinent to mention that the

MOD letter of 18 Nov 1996 was issued between the dates of convening the Special Selection Board (31 Oct 1996) and declaration of its results. The order, therefore, prima facie seems discriminatory and malafide.

20. It is also pertinent to point out that this letter of 18 November 1996, is in fact an amendment to the original MOD letter No 18684/JS/(P&W)/86 dated 20 October 1986 which had laid down certain stipulations (in revision of the then existing stipulations) for appointment of Army Commanders/Vice Chief of the Army Staff. Such rulings are normally given a future date of applicability in order to safeguard career interests of those who immediately come under their purview. Even the earlier letter, which was issued on 20 October 1986, was made applicable with effect from 01 Jan 1988. Besides, the career interests of the affected officers were protected. However, in the case of 18 November 1996 letter making the stipulation applicable with immediate effect has violated this norm. This coupled with the fact of my deferment makes the new stipulation applicable to me almost retrospectively and places me in such a situation where no amount of hard and dedicated work can undo the adverse effect on my career prospects. Therefore, the new stipulation as laid down by the government is unfair, unjustified and legally incorrect.

21. It is learnt through the civil writ petition No 2667/1997 of Maj Gen H S Bagga versus the Union of India filed in the High Court of Delhi, New Delhi, that our results of the Selection Board of 31 Oct 1996 had actually been finalized by the competent authority and received by the MOD on 30 Nov 1996. However, the MOD (who received the results on 30 Nov 1996 itself)

did not declare the results as it asked for a review of the result of Maj Gen (now Lt Gen) BS Malik. Since there was no review sought in case of my results, logically my case should have been delinked from that of Maj Gen BS Malik and my result should have been declared. However, this was not done by the MOD, ultimately resulting in a further delay of three months in the declaration of my results. If my result (of having been deferred) had been declared by the MOD on 30 Nov 1996, there was every likelihood that the Army would have convened another Special Selection Board and I would have been approved, promoted and appointed Corps Commander before 01 Mar 1997, thus completing one year in the command of Corps before becoming due for appointment of Army Commander on 01 Mar 1998.

22. From the foregoing it would be seen that the adverse effect on my career is a cumulative effect of the following three actions of the government:

(a) I was 'deferred' by the government in the Special Selection Board held on 31 Oct 1996 for reasons not stated and still not intimated to me, which should have been done as per established procedure and precedence.

(b) Between the dates of convening the Special Selection Board on 31 Oct 1996 and declaration of its results, the government introduced a new stipulation that henceforth an officer should command a Corps for at least one year before becoming eligible for appointment of Army Commander. This stipulation has been made applicable from the date of issue of the government letter of 18 Nov 1996 and no lead-time has been given which is contrary to precedence in similar cases.

(c) My results of the Special Selection Board held on 31 Oct 1996 were delayed for three months for no apparent reason as these results had already been finalized by the competent authority (on 30 Nov 1996) and no review of my result was either in progress or contemplated. This delay effectively ensured that I would not complete commanding a Corps for one year before a vacancy of Army commander occurred (on 01 Mar 1998) for which my merit and seniority make me eligible.

Prayer

23. In view of the foregoing I request that:

(a) The grading 'deferred' awarded to me by the government during the 31 October 1996 Selection Board may please be reviewed and I be considered approved and deemed to have been placed in command of a Corps retrospectively from the date of declaration of the results of that Selection Board.

(b) If above is not possible, the stipulation of commanding a Corps for minimum one year to become eligible for appointment as an Army commander issued vide MOD letter No 19/(24)/96/ D(MS) dated 18 November 1996 be waived in my case, as the delay in my promotion has been caused entirely in the interest of Service.

(c) Any other suitable relief be provided to protect my career interests from adverse effect of unjustified and illegal decisions.

The complaint, addressed to the Government of India, was routed through the chain of command and had to be processed through the COAS. The summary of comments given by the MS Branch on the files fully validates my plea that I had no control over my delayed repatriation and is reproduced below:

"Hence, prima facie it appears that the delay in repatriation has been caused due to organizational constraints and not by individual requirement. Subsequent events of his promotion to the rank of Maj Gen and consideration for the next promotion and placement were all affected by this inordinate delay, thus bringing him now under the debar clause.

Keeping in view—it will be unfair and a total denial of natural justice, if the Gen Offr is not considered for promotion to the appt of Army Cdr, by excluding him under the clause of MOD letter No 19(24)/96/D(MS) dt 18 Nov 96. The denial of consideration will tantamount to double punishment by the organization to an individual for no fault of his own, the 'raison d'etre' being delayed repatriation from France.

For promotion to the rank of Lt Gen Offr is required to command a Div or equivalent for a period of 18 months and earn 2 reports therefrom. MS however is empowered to grant waiver in the tenure. The 1962 batch of Gen Cadre to which the complainant belongs, was considered for promotion to the rank of Lt Gen in Oct 94, Apr 95, Oct 96 and Apr 97, as number of offrs were large and all were not "adequately Exercised" together. As the complainant took over the criteria appointment in the rank of Maj Gen on 03 Sep 95, he was not AE and his case was successively deferred till Apr 96 by the SSB. For SSB held on 31 Oct 96 the Gen Offr had a shortfall of 4 months 3 days in tenure. Under the existing policy MS granted waiver and the Gen Offr was duly considered by the SSB. Because of the organizational requirement, most of the officers were considered after they had done a tenure of about 15 months and in one case even 14 months. Similar waivers were given to the offrs of other batches of Gen Cadre and supporting arms and services. Ministry of Defence had always accepted the waivers granted by MS. Some of the comparable waivers earlier granted are mentioned below:

Name of the Officer	***Batch***	***Shortfall in AE period***
(a) GS Brar, GC	*1961*	*3 months 28 days*
(b) BN Kapur, GC	*1961*	*3 months 26 days*
(c) RK Sawhney, GC	*1961*	*3 months 29 days*
(d) Gurpreet Singh, GC	*1962*	*4 months*
(e) PK Puri, GC	*1962*	*3 months 4 days*
(f) SC Chopra, GC	*1962*	*3 months 5 days*
(g) MPS Bhandari Arty (for staff bd)	*1961*	*4 months 6 days*
(h) PS Modak, Sigs (for Staff Bd)	*1961*	*4 months*

On the basis of consideration given in Oct 96, the complainant was recommended 'B' Fit grading by the Special Selection Board. Maj Gen BS Malik who was also considered in the Board as Special Review (Fresh) case was recommended 'Z' (unfit) grading. While processing the Selection Board proceedings, MOD inter-alia raised observation on waiver of period to the complainant, which was adequately explained by citing the precedent cases also. MOD, however, revised the grading 'Fit' to 'deferred' in case of the complainant without assigning any reasons and that of Maj Gen BS Malik from Z (unfit) to B (Fit). The Gen offr was subsequently considered in Apr 97 and was approved as 'Fit' for promotion to the rank of Lt Gen in Jul 97.

It is also pertinent to bring out that law of equity suggests that all offrs of one batch should be subjected to same terms and conditions of service. Keeping this aspect in mind any change of policy should provide in-built career protection by the management in terms of a lead-time. This was done when MOD issued letter No 18684/JS(P&W)/86 dated 20 Oct 86 – the provisions of this letter were made applicable wef 01 Jan 88. Also to cater for the cases of offrs who were being affected, a provision for pay protection was provided vide Para 1 (d) of the letter. However, in the MOD letter No 19(24)/96/D(MS) dated 18 Nov 96 no such provision except for grant of waiver with the concurrence of the Government has been provided. This clause of grant of waiver with the concurrence of the Government is a restrictive clause and 'ipso facto' unfortunately applies only to Lt Gen RS Kadyan, VSM, in 1962 batch, due to his inordinately delayed placement in command of a Corps. If the criteria as laid down in Nov 96 letter had a lead time as done in the 20 Oct 86 letter, the Gen Offr would have been considered for appointment of GOC-in-C without any encumbrances.

It is also seen that in the recent past prior to issue of MOD letter No 19(24)/96/D(MS) dated 18 Nov 96, following Gen Offrs with less than one year as Corps Commander were promoted as Army Cdrs:

	Tenure as Corps Cdr (in months)	***Period covered by CR when considered for Army Cdr***
(a) Gen Roychowdhury, PVSM	*10 ½*	*Not known since CRD with MOD*
(b) Lt Gen Jameel Mahmood, UYSM	*07 ½*	*4 months*
(c) Lt Gen A Gautam, PVSM	*08 ½*	*5 months & 10 days*
(d) Lt Gen SK Sharma, PVSM, AVSM	*11*	*5 months*

In view of the above detailed examination of the case, CAB is of the view that Lt Gen RS Kadyan, VSM, be granted waiver of six months in tenure of GOC 1 Corps and considered for the appointment of GOC-in-C Eastern Command as the Gen Offr is not completing AE criteria due to :

- *(a) Delayed repatriation from France resulting in*
- *(b) Delayed placement on criteria appointment in the rank of Maj Gen*
- *(c) Delayed consideration for promotion to the rank of Lt Gen and*
- *(d) Revision of 'fit' grading to 'Deferred', which resulted in*
- *(e) Further delay in consideration, approval and placement as GOC Corps, and*
- *(f) Application of new clause vide MOD letter of 18 Nov 96, the provisions of which only exclude him in 1962 batch vis-à-vis his batch mates.*

All the above events were beyond the control of the complainant and were basically caused by the administrative constraints of the organization. Hence, the Gen Offr deserves the benefit of grant of waiver in terms of natural justice and equal rights, clause of the law.

The Army also sought the legal opinion from the Judge Advocate General (JAG) of the Army on the subject of grant of waiver to me. The JAG, who is a Maj Gen, is the seniormost officer of the Army's legal branch. Lt Gen Kalkat who was commanding a Corps and who stood to gain in case my complaint was rejected, was obviously keeping himself well informed on the progress of my statutory complaint. It is interesting to know that during this period Kalkat rang up the JAG, and pleaded that since the former's own father had also served in the JAG department, the JAG should have natural affinity while examining the case. It is a sad commentary that a serving Lt Gen considered it appropriate to speak to a junior officer, invoking his own father's connection, and seeking his help in bringing harm to the career interests of a colleague. Ambition does blind some of us.

On 06 January 1998 the Chief of the Army Staff sent the following note to the Ministry of Defence:

1. *I have perused the Statutory Complaint dated 05 Oct 97 against supersession in respect of IC-13153H Lt Gen RS Kadyan, VSM, Inf, and examined the same against his overall profile and other relevant documents.*
2. *After consideration of all aspects of the complaint and having examined it against all documents and happenings, I am of the opinion that the Gen Offr would have been considered for the appointment of Army Cdr/VCOAS in normal circumstances had he not been inordinately delayed in being placed on present criteria appointment. On detailed examination I find that delay caused was due to circumstances well beyond the control of the Gen Offr and were primarily due to administrative constraints of the organization. I also find that new clause of tenure of one year as a Corps Cdr affects only the Gen Offr vis-à-vis his batch mates basically due to delayed placement.*
3. *In view of the above, I recommend that redress be granted to the Gen Offr by way of granting 6 months AE waiver to him for consideration for promotion to the appointment of Army Cdr/VCOAS for a vacancy occurring on 01 Mar 98.*

An important point that needs to be noted and that is relevant to what happened subsequently in the Supreme Court, is that nowhere in my Statutory Complaint had I mentioned any specific period for which the waiver was required. I had merely asked that, *the stipulation of commanding a Corps for minimum one year to become eligible for appointment as an Army commander issued vide MOD letter No 19/(24)/ 96/ D(MS) dated 18 November 1996 be waived in my case.* The Chief of the Army Staff had quantified the waiver to the specific period of 6 months after taking into consideration - as was blindingly obvious - the fact that my experience of command of the Corps had commenced on 23 August 1997, even though the first one month of that command was in the rank of Maj Gen. Taking that date as the basis, I would have had 6 months and 7 days of command on the date of vacancy of Army Commander i.e. 01 March 1998. If 6 months waiver was added to it, I would be deemed to have commanded the Corps for 1 year and 7 days thus meeting the requirement of command of a Corps for minimum 1 year as laid down vide Government letter dated 18 November 1996. The Army Chief left no doubt or vagueness by specifying the date of vacancy of the Army Commander's post. He recommended '*...6 months AE waiver* to him for consideration for promotion to the appointment of Army Cdr/VCOAS *for a vacancy occurring on 01 Mar 98*'. (Emphasis added).

I continued commanding 1 Corps. In the normal course my ACR would have been due on 01 July 1998. However, the Army Headquarters asked for a special report covering the period up to 31 January 1998. It was initiated by the Army Commander Central Command as the IO on 08 February 1998. The COAS visited my Corps on 26 and 27 February 1998, to witness a Corps War Game that had been scheduled. He departed from my headquarters in the afternoon of Friday, 27 February 1998, and the same evening, after return to New Delhi, he wrote my report in the capacity of the RO.

As already mentioned the ACR forms for officers up to the rank of Maj Gen have a provision for award of numerical grades for various traits so as to permit comparison during selection boards. After an officer becomes a Lt Gen there are no more selection boards and hence the ACR consists of a simple pen picture and recommendations for employment/ promotion. The reports written on me by the IO and the RO are given below:

Report by the IO, Lt Gen Surjit Singh, GOC-in-C, Central Command on 8 February 1998:

> *A smart, trim newly promoted Lt Gen who has commanded his Corps with competence. Professionally sound and aware he has perceptive outlook. Kadian understands fluid situations and takes appropriate actions – keeps well abreast of developments. Is creative in conceptualisation and resolution. Socially pleasant and a good mixer.*

Report by the RO, Gen VP Malik, Chief of the Army Staff, on 27 February 1998:

> *A smart officer with all soldierly traits. Is straight forward and goes by the work. Establishes good rapport with subordinate and peers. Professionally competent, he is systematic, goes into details, and is aware of the politico-military environment. Kadyan has handled Corps well so far.*

In the portion dealing with 'Employment and Fitness for Promotion', the IO and the RO had to answer the following two questions with a simple 'yes' or 'no':

(a) *Do you consider him fit in every way to hold his present rank?* The answer by both is 'yes'.

(b) *Do you consider him fit for promotion to the next higher rank/appointment?* Again the answer by both, the IO as well as the RO is 'yes'.

There was a well-timed article that appeared in *The Indian Express* on 27 February 1998 when the COAS was in my headquarters. In bold headlines the front-page article said, *'Sensitive Eastern Command headless as Government dithers over posting'.* The sub heading was, *'Contender, a Brigadier until 1995, has filed a complaint seeking 'special dispensation' (read favours), MoD wastes time listening'.* The article by Manvendra Singh, quoted details from my complaint. Obviously the reporter had got access to it. Its timing was undoubtedly intended to influence the COAS in writing my report. The newspaper report was apparently inspired by someone who had access to my complaint and who knew in detail the schedule of the visit of the COAS.

I took leave during March 1998. The Army circles were agog with rumours of all kinds. I have never given credence to rumours and I decided to seek an audience with the COAS himself.

On 05 March 1998, I met the COAS in his office. I urged on him that if he found something lacking in me professionally, he was welcome to appoint the officer next in seniority. However, otherwise the clearly laid out orders and well established precedent of appointing the seniormost fit officer to the post must be followed. I also impressed on him that he should withhold sending his recommendations till the Ministry took a final decision on my statutory complaint seeking a waiver. I did not know, nor did the Army Chief tell me, that he had already sent his recommendations on 02 March 1998.

Many friends told me later that during my meeting I should also have told the Army Chief that I would go to court in case my due was denied to me. But my training and the Army culture that I had imbibed over the years could not have permitted me even to think of issuing any kind of a 'threat' to the Chief of the Army Staff.

As brought out, I did not know at the time of my meeting with the Army Chief that he had already sent his recommendations on 2 March 1998 without waiting for the decision on my statutory complaint, and thus on my eligibility vis-a-vis one year command of a Corps. In this he had recommended name of a junior, Lt Gen HRS Kalkat for the post of Eastern Army Commander. This was strange. On Friday evening, 27 February, after witnessing my performance in the war game the Army Chief finds me fit for promotion to the next higher rank and fit for appointment in that rank. For a Lt Gen the only next higher rank is that of Gen and in that rank the only appointment is that of the Chief of the Army Staff. Thus on Friday evening he found me fit for promotion to the rank of Gen and on Monday morning he recommended my super- session for the appointment of Army Commander. The compelling reason for this somersault over the weekend would only be known to Gen Malik, the then Chief of Army Staff. However, prima facie his action cannot be explained in any rational manner. But let me revert to this later.

March 1998 was a momentous month for me. First, some helpful souls in the ministry told me that the Minister had already promised a prominent Punjab politician from a Left party that Kalkat would be appointed the Army Commander and therefore, there was no question of granting me a waiver. This may partly explain why my request for a waiver recommended by the Army Chief on 06 January 1998, and intended specifically for the Army Commander's vacancy occurring on 01 March 1998, was not decided till after that date of vacancy, and till after the Army Chief had made his recommendation.

Now that the Army Chief had made his recommendation, the Ministry decided to wash their hands and 'trap' the Army Chief into being answerable to any questions that might later arise on the subject. Having received the 2 March recommendations of the Army Chief, the Ministry now raised three queries vide their note dated 05 March 1998. One of these queries pertained to the delay in forwarding the recommendations for the appointment of Army Commander. Why did the Chief send his recommendations so late when the occurrence of the vacancy was clearly foreseen and there had been many reports in the media about it? To this Gen Malik replied that a major war game had been planned in 1 Corps in end February and he wanted to see my performance before writing my report. He of course did not explain as to why after seeing that performance and finding me fit for promotion to the next higher rank in his report, did he still recommend a junior's name and by implication my super-session. If he had to do that then where was the need to delay his recommendations till after the war game? The Ministry could have raised this point but since Gen Malik's recommendation was fitting into their scheme of things, it was convenient for them not to pursue the matter.

The second query was the Ministry's observation that in the past only seniormost officer found fit had been appointed Army commander and this time a departure was being made. Could the Army Chief cite precedents where the seniormost fit officer was not appointed? Gen Malik had no truthful answer to this query, because never before, since the issue of the 20 October 1986 Government letter, had the seniormost officer found fit in all respects been denied the post. Therefore – and it saddens me to state this - the Army Chief resorted to a falsehood in answering this query. In his note dated 06 March 1998, he cited names of Lt Gens IJ Khanna, Maya Dass and GL Bakshi who though seniormost were not appointed Army commanders based - in Malik's words - 'on comparative merit and weak profile'. Gen Malik could not have been unaware that these three Lt Gens were denied the post because in their ACR as Corps Commanders all these three had negative recommendation regarding their fitness for promotion. Therefore, they were not 'fit' in every respect as required by Government letter dated 20 October 1986. There was no question of their coming in comparative merit since they did not fulfil the eligibility criteria of fitness. **The Chief of the Army Staff, who is a repository of the faith of a million plus men in uniform, belied that faith and resorted to falsehood to support his wrong and unjustified recommendation.**

Was it possible that Gen Malik might have been genuinely convinced that the post of Army Commander is a selection post that entails comparative merit? In the interest of upholding the dignity of the office of the COAS, I personally would have preferred that to be the case. But unfortunately, the fact that Gen Malik had no doubt that the post of Army Commander was not a selection post, can be proved by another documentary evidence.

On being commissioned, Gen VP Malik had passed out 37th in the order of merit in his course. This was by no means an achievement that could foretell his rise to the highest post and rank. What took him there were his younger age, sheer luck, and some chance developments. After commanding a Corps, he was posted as Commandant of Staff College in Wellington, because based on the then foreseen vacancies of Army Commanders and his seniority, he was not in the run to become an Army Commander. (Since the post of Army Commander is always filled based on the principle of seniority-cum-fitness, it is a matter of simple mathematical calculation to work out who would and who would not reach that post). He would have retired on 1 November 1997 from either that post in Wellington or some other equivalent post. Unfortunately, the then Army Chief Gen BC Joshi died in harness on 18 November 1994. In his place the next seniormost Lt Gen Shankar Roychowdhury was promoted to the rank of Gen and was appointed the Army Chief on 21 November 1994 . This created a chain vacancy of an Army Commander. This was to go to Lt Gen KL (Kevin) D'Souza who was then the seniormost Lt Gen. D'Souza was of the same batch as Lt Gen Malik but was higher than Malik in seniority. The Lt Gen next in seniority to D'Souza was Lt Gen SK Sharma who was also of the same batch but senior to Malik. Therefore, after this vacancy (caused by Gen Joshi's demise) was filled up by Lt Gen D'Souza, SK Sharma would take the next vacancy that was to occur on 1 July 1995. By the time a next vacancy of an Army Commander occurred (after 01 July 1995), Malik would have become ineligible in view of the two years residual service rule. Thus, even though Gen Joshi's demise brought him a notch closer to the post of Army Commander, it still was not close enough. But his ambition put him in overdrive.

While the Army was still in mourning over the tragic demise of one of its most dynamic and visionary Chiefs, on the sixth day of the tragedy, on 24 November 1994, Lt Gen Malik, wrote a letter to the newly appointed Army Chief, Gen Roychowdhury. In this he clearly conceded that the first vacancy that had already occurred would go to Lt Gen KL D'Souza and the next one on 01 July 1995, would go to Lt Gen SK Sharma. Both these vacancies, as per Malik's own contention, were to go to these officers because of their seniority and fitness. Malik made no claim to the first or the second of these vacancies based on the hypothetical basis that in comparison he, though junior, might have been found more suitable. Nor did he concede that the third vacancy might go to someone junior to him because such junior may be found better than Malik in comparison. I am highlighting this to make the point that Gen Malik was very much aware of, and never questioned the policy that the post of Army Commander is not a selection post and is given to the seniormost officer found fit for the post. In this letter Malik clearly conceded this point. Later, when he himself became Chief and was placed in a position where he had to make recommendations in my case, he made it out that the Army Commander's post was a selection post. **I am constrained to point out that this was a display of double standards by the Chief of the Army Staff.** And to support his recommendation (which he knew was against his own conviction, contrary to existing orders and had no precedent), he cited names of three Lt Generals knowing full well that it was false and that these three officers had not been appointed Army Commanders simply because they had a negative recommendation in their ACRs as Corps Commanders, and were thus not 'fit' in every respect and were therefore not eligible for consideration. In their case there was no question of any comparison.

The Ministry of Defence could of course have challenged the false statement by the Army Chief in his Note dated 6 March 1998. The Joint Secretary dealing with the case did in fact point out on the file that Lt Gen IJ Khanna, Mayadas and GL Bakshi were actually passed over because they had a negative recommendation in their ACRs as Corp Commanders and not because of comparative merit as stated by the Army Chief, but did nothing to send this back to the Army Chief seeking clarification. Nor was this anomaly set right by the seniormost bureaucrat in the Ministry i.e. the Defence Secretary who at the time was Ajit Kumar, an IAS officer from the Punjab cadre.

While making a false statement on the file Gen Malik could not of course have been unaware that the Ministry of

Defence has all the records and would know the statement to be false. If despite this a person of the level of the Chief of Army Staff makes a factually incorrect statement, it is safe to assume that there may have existed some kind of a collusion or understanding between the two authorities.

As a third query in their note dated 05 March 1998, the Ministry asked the Army Chief whether he would change his mind if the waiver (on my statutory complaint) were now granted. What was the Chief expected to do? If he said that a waiver would in fact involve a change in his recommendation because it would make me also eligible, then he would contradict his recommendation (supposedly based on 'comparative' merit) sent barely three days ago. If he said that there would be no change, it suited the Ministry ideally. The Army Chief adopted the latter option.

Having received the reply (dated 6 March 1998) from the Army Chief, the bureaucrats now cleaned their slate. After getting a confirmation that the name recommended was indeed that of Kalkat, they now granted me the waiver on 16 March 1998. It needs to be noted that on 16 March when the waiver was finally granted, it had ceased to have any meaning. Kalkat's name had already been recommended and it was irrelevant whether a waiver was granted to me or not.

I would like to quote another incident to throw light on what goes on behind the scenes in the 'fair' system of senior Army appointments.

The Bribe

Brig YP Goyal had been commanding the Rajputana Rifles Regimental Centre in Delhi Cantonment till 31 January 1998, when he retired. Since we belong to the same Regiment and I was in fact the Colonel of the Rajputana Rifles, he was fully familiar with the details of what was happening regarding my waiver and the appointment as Army Commander. Some time in the second week of March 1998 he told me that the previous evening he had hosted a bureaucrat serving in the Ministry of Defence and his wife for dinner in his house and that it would be useful if I also met them. On getting my concurrence, he arranged another dinner in his house two days later where he called the same bureaucrat couple and me along with my wife. During the evening the bureaucrat's wife and I had a chat standing in one corner of the drawing room. She had an interesting advice on how I could become an Army Commander. She told me that for the 01 March 1998 vacancy Kalkat was becoming the Army Commander and I should not challenge it. Subsequently, I should put up a statutory complaint seeking a waiver of one month's shortfall in the required two years residual service for the next vacancy occurring on 01 October 1998. She assured me that her husband would ensure grant of that waiver to me. For a finale she coolly added that it would cost me Rs five lakhs! Naturally this was absolutely unacceptable to me and has been recounted only to reveal an alternative channel for promotions in existence.

As I mentioned earlier, March 1998 was a momentous month. My long-held belief and faith in the fairness of the Army's system, the highest regard and respect for the person who occupied the chair of the COAS, the repeatedly drilled-into-me notion that our system was free from political interference and that we prided ourselves in strict adherence to rules, all came crashing down. I was not clear what my next step should be. I decided to approach the Army Chief again. After the waiver was granted to me on 16 March 1998, I wrote to the COAS on 21 March. In this communication I mentioned that with the grant of the waiver I have now met all the conditions of eligibility and the existing rule of appointing Army Commanders based on seniority and fitness may please be followed. Extracts of the letter are reproduced as follows:

2. *It is learnt that my statutory complaint has since been disposed of by the Government and a waiver has been granted from the requirement of commanding a Corps for at least one year before becoming eligible for appointment of Army Commander. It could not have been possible without your support and blessings and I wish to record my deep gratitude.*
3. *As far as I know, the seniormost eligible officer has always been appointed Army Commander subject to his being found fit in all other respects as prescribed. This has been in consonance with the established convention and ethos of the Indian Army. As known there has been no exception to this rule.*
4. *For the last three years I have been put to great inconvenience but the system has always stood by me and has ensured fairness, which alone has enabled me to rise to this level. I have full faith in your sense of fairness and having come so close to becoming an Army Commander, I am confident that you will get justice for me.*
5. *With the grant of the waiver, one of the eligibility conditions for becoming an Army Commander is met. I am also the seniormost among eligible Lt Gens. If I am found meeting all other conditions, may I request that I may kindly be considered for the post lying vacant since 01 Mar 98.*
6. *Assuring you of my complete and unflinching loyalty to the Army and to our value system.*

To set the record straight, it needs to be clarified that all the exchange of notes between the Army Chief and the Ministry mentioned earlier became known to me much later. I have mentioned these here only to give a chronological sequence to the narration. On 21 March 1998, when I wrote the above letter to Gen Malik I was not even aware that he had already sent his recommendation on 2 March 1998.

My statutory complaint was disposed of by granting me a waiver on my alternative prayer vide Government of India Order No 16(8)/ 98/D (MS) dated 16 March 1998. Besides being given at a time when it had already become redundant, the reason for not granting me my main prayer is interesting. It reads :

The Central Government have considered the statutory complaint of Lt. Gen. RS Kadyan (IC-13153) Inf, against Govt. decision about 'deferred' grading awarded to him in the Oct. 96 Spl Selection Board.

> *After going through the facts of the case and the recommendation of the COAS, it is considered that the arguments furnished by the General officer against the award of 'deferred' grading to him are not tenable. The fact that for the period of his stay on deputation at Paris, the officer must have furnished 'adverse career certificate' has been taken into consideration and hence it is considered that his late promotions to the higher ranks were in order and were in no way discriminatory, unfair or malafide against him. However, it is also noted that at the time of giving the 'adverse career certificate', the stipulation of 1 year minimum service as Corps Cdr for promotion to the rank of Army Cdr/VCOAS was not there and hence the officer could not have taken that into account. In the light of the same and to meet the ends of justice, the Central Government in consonance with the prayer of the officer in para 23 (b) and the recommendation of the COAS agrees to grant him waiver of six months in terms of Ministry of Defence letter No 19(24)/96/ D(MS) of 18th Nov 96 for his consideration for promotion to the rank of Army Cdr/VCOAS.*

When the Government arbitrarily changed my grading from 'fit' to 'deferred', in their Note dated 23 November 1996, put up to the ACC, they had mentioned the three grounds i.e. a special report had been called for in my case, that I had completed inadequate time in the criteria appointment (11 months is what they had falsely stated) and that my second report was initiated by the RO. Writing of such 'grounds' in their never-to-be-seen-by-others confidential files (and no one would have known of these if I had not gone to court), was a safe bet for the government. But in the waiver order, that had to be communicated to me, these 'grounds' were too flimsy. So, they had to come up with fresh lies to reject my main prayer. What exactly did they mean when they said I 'must have furnished adverse career certificate'? The government had and still has all the documents and files in their possession. How could they use the expression *'must have'* for something, which is verifiable?

It is true that I had used this speculative 'must have' in my statutory complaint. Let me explain. When I departed for Paris in November 1990, I had sent my unwanted baggage to my native village in Haryana. On return, I was posted in Nagaland and there was no time or occasion or even need for that baggage in a field area. I collected it only in end 1997 after being posted to Mathura. When I wrote my statutory complaint on 5 October 1997, I still had not collected the baggage, which included my old files. I was therefore not sure whether I gave such a certificate, in which case an office copy would be in my files. Since an adverse career certificate, even if furnished, remains operative only for the normal tenure of 3 years (and not for 4 years and 9 months that I was kept in Paris), I did not consider it relevant enough for the purposes of seeking a waiver and used the speculative term 'must have furnished' in my complaint. After I collected my old files I learnt that no such certificate had indeed been given. However, notwithstanding what I wrote, it is unusual for the government to issue a government letter and reject my main prayer based on a false premise. They fully knew that no such certificate had been furnished.

The hard fact is that no adverse career certificate was ever asked for or given. This was in consonance with the Military Secretary's policy at the time of my proceeding abroad on posting and there was nothing shady about it. And the Government was fully aware of it. There cannot be any 'must have' in this matter. In a flagrant misuse of their powers, the government rejected my main prayer on a false ground. And as an aggrieved party I could do nothing against the might of the government.

As would be seen, my stay in Paris was the main reason for my less than 18 months of AE period for the 31 October 1996 Selection Board, supposedly resulting in my grading being changed from 'fit' to 'deferred', and finally to my curtailed tenure as Corps Commander when I became due for the Army Commander's post necessitating my seeking a waiver in which my main prayer was rejected on false and untenable grounds. Despite this before the Delhi High Court the Government took a contrary view. This is what the Hon'ble Judge had to observe in the judgment:

> *However, learned Solicitor General, Mr. Santosh Hegde, appearing for the respondents, categorically stated that his tenure at Paris has got no adverse impact to deny the petitioner his promotion as Army Commander...*

Mr. Ranjit Sethi had been the Ambassador in France during the last two years of my tenure there. He was fully aware of the circumstances under which my term as Military Attaché got extended. In fact before leaving Paris I had apprised him of my apprehension that my extended stay in Paris might come in way of my career progression. He had kept himself informed of the developments. Being himself the son of an Army officer, he could comprehend the system of Army's functioning. In 1997, he wrote two letters on the subject to the concerned bureaucrats in Delhi. On 12 November 1997, he wrote to the Defence Secretary, Ajit Kumar. The letter read :

> *I am writing to you with regard to the posting to Paris of the former Military Attaché, Raj Kadyan, Brigadier at the time and now Lieutenant General.*
>
> *He stayed in Paris beyond the normal period of three years.*
>
> *I feel morally obliged to explain the circumstances, as I believe that the longer than usual stay in Paris has proved to be a handicap for him.*
>
> *I must at the outset assert that Kadyan's extended stay in Paris was not of his own doing or desire. First, his move got mixed up with the maintenance of the post of Military attaché.*
>
> *Later, I intervened for him to stay until his successor arrived. Of course, I as Ambassador also had a role in preserving the post in Paris earlier.*
>
> *My case on both counts was substantive. During the period in question, we had serious defence matters to deal with and be informed about. The Military Attaché was then vital. This was so notably – and I feel that it is useful that I mention this – with regard to the French defence relationship with.... It was important for us to have somebody able to track down, elicit and analyse information on French military supplies to.... This information became vital for our diplomatic work and*

reactions, as you would recall particularly with regard to the supply to... of....

I feel that I need not extensively describe the requirement for a Military Attaché. The fact is that Kadyan became subject – I hesitate to use the word victim – of circumstances. He constantly stated his need to return to India in his professional interest.

I would earnestly suggest that the facts be considered, particularly in dealing with Kadyan's further career and promotions. I do not know the details but the fact of his staying in Paris beyond the normal term should not be treated as a privilege, rather a circumstance in the line of duty.

(Blanks inserted by author in the interest of guarding confidentiality of the strategic issues).

Ambassador Ranjit Sethi also wrote on 17 November 1997, to Shri NN Vohra, the then Principal Secretary to Prime Minister. This letter read:

I am writing about the former Military Attaché in this Mission, Raj Kadyan. You might have known him at the Defence Ministry.

His case has caused me some concern, mainly because of the possible effects on his prospects of promotion and career advancement of his prolonged stay in Paris.

In brief, he stayed on in Paris for longer than his three-year term for two reasons. The first was that his move got enmeshed with the future of the post of Military attaché. A decision to abolish the post had been initiated. I opposed it, as the Attaché has always fulfilled an important role in this Embassy. We have an important defence relationship with France. In addition, we need to be vigilant about ... relationship with this country. This is quite apart from European defence developments, NATO and other factors.

While the question of the future of the Military Attaché was being considered, inevitably Kadyan was maintained in his post.

Later, after the future of the post was secured, there was a further delay pending the choice of his successor. It was not possible to be without a Military Attaché, particularly as there were significant developments at the time in France's defence relationship with.... This involved the supply of both...and...as you would recall. We needed to be, and were, very active in regard to developments at the time. The Military Attaché's role was crucial.

Raj Kadyan never sought to stay in Paris beyond his three-year term. This is fully documented. He wanted to get back to India for command appointments. Indeed, his stay in Paris entailed some sacrifices. It was not an undue privilege.

I am writing to you as it would appear that Kadyan's further advancement could be jeopardized because of his extended stay in Paris. This would be unfortunate.

Kadyan is at the moment commanding 1 Corps. He should be in line for an Army Command. It was only casually that I learned that there may be complications, linked to his Paris posting.

I have already written to Defence Secretary about his case. I thought I would also refer to you. I feel morally obliged to explain the circumstances of Kadyan's later stay in Paris, so that he is not unduly penalized.

(Blanks inserted by the author to maintain confidentiality of contents)

The New Angle

Ranjit Sethi had retired on 01 March 1998, and had arrived in Delhi. We had been in touch. He knew that my extended tenure in France was proving a handicap. He felt morally responsible; while he had not intervened to have me stay longer at the post, and I had repeatedly expressed my wish to return, I had been held up because the whole question of the abolition of the post of military attaché had been opened up at his insistence. He had clarified this in correspondence with both the civil and military offices in South Block prior to his return on retirement in March 1998. On his return he took it upon himself to take up the matter with the authorities, recalling the letters he had written earlier. Among those he met, soon after his return in March was Jaswant Singh, who had just been made the Deputy Chairman of the Planning Commission, following his failure to get elected to the Lok Sabha. Sethi knew Jaswant Singh personally and felt confident that as a man of experience of the military, he would grasp the issues at stake. Jaswant Singh heard Sethi out with attention and even suggested that he see George Fernandes, who had just taken over the Defence portfolio. In the course of their conversation Jaswant Singh mentioned some undefined complications on account of Kalkat being a Sikh adding that there was widespread concern that no Sikh had ever been appointed Chief of Army Staff. The suggestion that the appointment of Kalkat was some sort of partial compensation was not precisely spelt out, but seemed implicit. The conversation tended to reveal a concern on the part of the Party leadership, in the political landscape of the time, which was dominated by the needs of the coalition, regarding Sikh sensitivities.

Sethi's later meeting with George Fernandes was apparently bland. When he finally met him, after a long wait at his Parliament House office, the minister gave Sethi a cursory hearing and said simply that the matter seemed difficult. Sethi was somewhat discouraged by his meetings, and confessed to me that in his retired state he felt there was little more he could do, notwithstanding the strength of his conviction that my stay in France should not be made a liability damaging my service interests.

The revelation about the sensitivity towards there having been no Sikh appointed as Army Chief left me stunned. My first reaction was of disbelief. I could not believe this was true. However, since it came from such a senior party ideologue as Jaswant Singh, and was conveyed to me through such a responsible person as an Ambassador, there was no chance of any misunderstanding or misinterpretation. True, the issue at stake was not an appointment of an Army Chief but an Army Commander, but the very fact that the 'sensitivity' was mentioned in this context, the two could not but be interlinked.

It may be relevant to recall that around mid-March 1998, there was a change of government at the Centre and a coalition of Allies had come to power. Since a waiver had now been granted to me and the Appointments Committee of the Cabinet had not yet cleared the appointment, there was still time for ensuring that senior Army appointments are made as per rules and as per time-tested precedent. Unfortunately this new government was ruling on a very slim majority (they actually fell some time later). The support of every single MP mattered. One of the political parties supporting the Central government had a sizeable presence in the Parliament and was a part of this coalition government. My apprehension was that they could have put pressure on the government to appoint one of 'theirs' as the Army Commander. When one looks at later developments, where Air Marshal Sekhon was sent home in 2002 because his request to the Punjab Chief Minister seeking the latter's help in influencing the government to get him a desired post became public (as revealed through newspaper reports), the pieces seem to fall in place.

If the earlier actions of the Ministry of Defence had rudely shaken my beliefs and my faith in the fairness of the government in dealing with promotions and appointments in the higher echelons of the Army, the latest disclosure (through Ranjit Sethi) totally shattered those beliefs. **If there is one organization in the country that is totally secular in both thoughts and deeds, it is the Army. That is one of the reasons why the Army is the ultimate resource available with the nation to tackle various problems and the Army never fails. We in uniform never look at one another based on our religion, caste or community. Secularism is one of the strongest pillars of the strength of the Indian Army.** But the politicians can go down to any level to serve their political needs. The revelation amounted to introducing a system of 'reservation' in the Army.

It is not in the purview of this book to comment on why Sikhs, Jats, Rajputs, Marathas and some other communities have never produced an Army Chief since 1947 in spite of having sizeable representation in the Army. (Gen JJ Singh is the first Sikh to have taken over as Army Chief on 01 February 2005.) My only lament is that I was being made a scapegoat in the political game.

What options did I have?

I had exhausted all the legitimate means available to me. Since the Army Chief had already bent with the wind, I had to seriously examine the options now available to me. I was in the evening of my Army career. I had reached the second highest rank in the Army. **The post of Army Commander was only an appointment and not a promotion. The post was certainly higher in status but it would not change my rank or my retirement date.** There was therefore some logic and practicality in my accepting the fait accompli and get resigned to it. But somewhere deep down in my conscience there was a disturbing voice troubling me. Acceptance of the situation would imply a tacit agreement with what the government was doing and would make me a part of a 'corrupt' culture in the government. I had been trained in the Army ethos where in a fight, defeat is acceptable but surrender is always a disgrace. My accepting the situation without a fight would be surrender. I had to challenge it.

I had personally met the highest uniformed officer of the Army and had pleaded my case. Some may assume that I still had a channel in the form of the Supreme Commander of the Armed Forces, to seek redress of my grievance. That supposition would be true only in theory. It is interesting to know that no serving person of the defence forces has the right to address a communication directly to the Supreme Commander. One has to go 'through proper channel'. It would have been absurd for me to write to the Supreme Commander alleging wrongdoing by the Chief of the Army Staff and the government and then ask these same agencies to process and forward my communication to the addressee.

The only recourse available to me was through the courts. This was not an easy option. Apart from the monetary aspect I was apprehensive on another count. I was doubtful whether while fighting against the government I would get a fair deal. I asked myself, 'How can I fight against the government and get justice when the government controls the post retirement employment of the judges?' The question kept haunting me. However, despite this nagging apprehension, I had naïve faith in our judicial system and having exhausted all other options, I decided to take recourse to the courts.

After analysing, I made up my mind on the following aspects:

- I would fight against the government decision to appoint a junior to the post of Army Commander, ignoring rules and precedent on the subject.
- Despite what the government was doing I would not let it affect my own firm views on the Army's secular structure.
- I would neither let the government doings nor the legal case affect my work or my attitude towards any officer or class of officers or men in the Army.
- I would not make the communal angle the plank of my legal case nor disclose this information to others as long I was to be in uniform.

Having made up my mind and with no other option left I filed my writ petition in the Delhi High Court on 26 March 1998.

6

The Case in Delhi High Court

A young, upcoming lawyer, Mr. Viraj Datar, drafted my writ petition under the guidance of his senior advocate Mr. Madan Lokur. After I had made up my mind to challenge the government decision, I did not want to waste any time. By now I had learnt that Kalkat's name had already been recommended to the Appointments Committee of the Cabinet (ACC). If I were to go to court after he was appointed, it would be much more difficult to challenge it. I therefore wanted the petition to be filed at the earliest. Despite the short notice, the legal team did a commendable job and drafted a fine writ petition.

In the writ petition I had cited the following as respondents:

(a) Respondent 1 : Union of India

(b) Respondent 2 : Chief of Army Staff

(c) Respondent 3 : Military Secretary

(d) Respondent 4 : Lt Gen HRS Kalkat.

The writ petition ended in the following Prayer:

(a) Issue a writ of Mandamus or any other appropriate writ, order or direction, directing Respondents 1 to 3 to appoint the Petitioner as the Army Commander, Eastern Command with effect from 1.3.1998.

(b) Issue writ, order or direction quashing the decision of Respondent 1 appointing/promoting Respondent No 4 as Army Commander Eastern Command.

(c) Issue a writ of Mandamus or any other appropriate writ, order or direction, directing Respondent Nos 1 to 3, to make the appointment/promotion of the Petitioner to the post of Army Commander Eastern Command in accordance with the letter/instructions dated 20.10.1986 after giving to the Petitioner the benefit of the grant of waiver from the condition/ stipulation laid down in the letter/ instruction dated 18.11.1996.

(d) Issue a writ of certiorari or any other appropriate writ, order or direction calling for the records of the case and quashing the recommendation made by Respondent No 4 for the appointment/promotion to the post of Army Commander Eastern Command.

(e) Issue a writ of certiorari or any other appropriate writ, order or direction calling for the records of the Selection Board held on 31.10.1996 and the decision taken thereon by Respondent No 1 and after examining the same quashing the deferment of the case of the Petitioner as being arbitrary, unconstitutional and violative of Article 14 of the Constitution of India and further directing that the Petitioner be deemed to be promoted to the rank of Lt Gen with effect from 31.10.1996.

(f) Issue a writ of Mandamus and or order or direction calling for the records and setting aside the directions of Respondent No 1 rejecting prayer (a) of the statutory complaint dated 05.10.1997 filed by the Petitioner under Section 27 of the Army Act.

(g) Pass such order and further order (s) as this Hon'ble Court may deem fit and proper in the facts and circumstances of the present case.

The writ petition was heard in the Delhi High Court on 27 March 1998. Lt Gen HRS Kalkat chose not to defend himself, did not engage any separate lawyer and was fighting his case along with the government through their legal team. The Hon'ble Court admitted the case and while issuing show cause notice on the application for stay made the following order:

> *...It is made clear that if any appointment is made to the post of Army Commander (Eastern Command), the same shall be subject to the result of the writ petition...*

The Court also fixed 20 April 1998, as the next date of hearing. As a non-legal person on the face of it I felt happy that a condition was to be attached to the forthcoming appointment of Kalkat as Army Commander. But my legal advisers told me that in actual practice it meant little. They told me from experience that the government would not even file a reply for the next thirty months and would retire me out (on 31 August 2000) with the petition still pending.

Based on legal advice therefore, I moved the next higher level i.e. the Division Bench of the Delhi High Court. The High Court Bench heard the case on 03 April 1998. The advocate, Mr. Nagar, represented the government. On that day the government said that they had already made officiating arrangements for Army Commander Eastern Command. It may be noted that these officiating arrangements are made when the permanent incumbent is not present for whatever reason. Normally the person next in seniority in that organization is given the charge of the officiating appointment and he performs these duties in addition to the duties of his permanent assignment. The officiating appointment is temporary in nature and, apart from experience and monetary allowance for doing the duty, does not confer any lasting benefits on the person who holds such an appointment. He reverts to his permanent post whenever a permanent incumbent is appointed. My counsel accepted the fact of the officiating appointment. *Inter alia* he forcefully argued that unlike the civil services the Army officers carry their rank visibly on their uniform. Besides, they have to face the junior officers and men daily. Therefore, supersession of any kind in the Army has more visible and humiliating implications vis-à-vis in the civil sector.

Accepting our arguments the Division Bench passed the following order:

> *Before us, it is stated by Mr. Nagar on instructions that the statutory complaint of the appellant has been accepted and the condition imposed by 18.11.1996 letter has been waived and the effect of this is that command of a Corps requirement is not to be applied to the case of appellant before us.*
>
> *It is also stated before us that name of appellant and respondent No. 4 is before the Appointment Committee of Cabinet and the matter is being considered there. It is not disputed that respondent No. 4 is officiating as Army Commander, Eastern Command.*
>
> *We are of the view that in the facts and circumstances of the case, as the writ petition is to come up for hearing on 20.4.1998, till disposal of the writ petition, it would be appropriate that no appointment is made and respondent No.4 is permitted to continue in an officiating capacity.*

It is significant to note that right at the beginning, even before the High Court scheduled the first hearing, the government had accepted before the Division Bench that with the grant of the (six months) waiver, the condition of minimum command of a Corps for one year imposed vide

Government letter dated 18.11.1996, no longer applies to me. Since Kalkat was also contesting the case as part of the government, he too admitted this position. And this was a statement of fact and not a legal opinion that could be interpreted differently.

The government challenged the High Court Division Bench order and went to the next higher level i.e. the Supreme Court through filing a Special Leave Petition (SLP) on 07 April 1998. In this the Government stated the following falsehood:

> *The Respondent No. 1 was posted as Military Attaché Embassy of India, Paris, France for a period of three years which ended in 1993. The Respondent No. 1 got his tenure extended for about 21 months and stayed as Military Attaché till August, 1995.*

It should be noted that the Government already had on the file the observation of the Army Chief himself (dated 6.1.1998) that my extended stay in Paris was due to the administrative constraints of the organization and that I had no control over it. Therefore, it can be concluded that the falsehood stated in an affidavit to the Supreme Court was a deliberate one. It was intended to tarnish my military reputation by projecting me as an opportunist who first 'got' his foreign stay extended and was now demanding his right in career enhancement. It was obviously intended to cause prejudice against me in the minds of the readers, including the judges.

The case came up in the Supreme Court on 20 April 1998. The government knew that one of our arguments would be that the government is delaying the filing of a reply to the writ petition and thus the finalisation of the case. Therefore, on 18 April they filed their reply in the form of a Counter Affidavit (CA). This must be some sort of a record of the speed with which the government has ever filed a reply to a petition.

The Supreme Court (Corum: Hon'ble the Chief Justice, Hon'ble Mr. Justice LT Thomas and Hon'ble Mr. Justice OP Wadhwa) passed the following interim order:

> There shall be stay of operation of the impugned judgment of the High Court. List after four weeks.

However, during the hearings, the Supreme Court made it clear that the appointment made would be subject to the outcome of the writ petition, as was decided by the Hon'ble Delhi High Court. Accordingly, Kalkat was appointed Army Commander conditionally vide Army Headquarters Signal dated 20 April 1998. The Signal clearly stated that the appointment is subject to the outcome of the writ petition.

On 20 July 1998, the case came up again in the Supreme Court for final orders. Since the Court had already issued interim orders, nothing fresh was expected from the Supreme Court. Therefore, in order to save some money, I decided to dispense with a lawyer and decided to plead my own case. The Bench only allowed me a short time during which I was able to get a reassurance from the Court that Kalkat's appointment was conditional and subject to the outcome of the writ petition. The Supreme Court judgment dated 20 July 1998, read as under :

> *"Leave granted.*
>
> *These appeals are against the order of a Division Bench of the Delhi High Court dated 3rd April, 1998 passed in LPA No. 149/98 & C.M. Nos. 844 and 945/98 arising out of an interlocutory order of a learned Single Judge. We had stayed the operation of this order vide order dated 20th April, 1998. The effect of the said order was that as ordered by the learned Single Judge, the Union of India could go ahead and make an appointment to the post of Army Commander, Eastern Command. It is stated that respondent no. 4, Lt. General*

HRS Kalkat has thus been appointed. As ordered by the learned Single Judge, the appointment is subject to the result of the pending writ petition.

Since the appointment of Shri Kalkat as Army Commander, Eastern Command, thus made is subject to the result of the writ petition nothing further remains to be done by this Court. It would suffice now to dispose the appeals as they are. Ordered accordingly.

Let me narrate another interesting incident to give the reader an insight as to how the highest functionaries of the Army could make false statements in a routine manner.

I was commanding 1 Corps when I filed my writ petition. On the staff of every Corps Headquarters there is an officer of the rank of Colonel from the Army's Judge Advocate General's department. His designation is Deputy Judge Advocate General (DJAG). He is posted to deal with all legal matters of the Corps as an organization. Since mine was an individual case, I did not feel it morally right to involve my DJAG. Therefore, I got my petition drafted, typed and prepared through civil sources. My DJAG learnt of it through his counterpart in Headquarters Western Command, who himself had come to know of it officially since Delhi as a station falls in the territorial jurisdiction of Western Command and all cases of Army personnel coming up in the Delhi courts get processed through them. In fact my DJAG took it as an indicator of my lack of confidence in his abilities, and was understandably upset. However, when I apprised him of my thinking on the subject, he appeared satisfied.

When the court case had gone through a few hearings, I noticed that the DJAG of 33 Corps – where Kalkat was/had been the Corps Commander – was present at every hearing. Therefore, on 27 April 1998, I wrote a letter to the Adjutant General, Lt Gen SS Grewal:

1. In the Supreme Court hearing on 20 Apr 98 concerning my writ petition, I saw Col MS Jaswal, Deputy Judge Advocate General, HQ 33 Corps, in military uniform taking part in the proceedings along with the Government Standing Counsel and representatives of other Respondents. The officer was assisting his then Corps Commander in the legal case....
2. This is to inform you that I have also decided to utilize the services of my Deputy Judge Advocate General in a similar manner with immediate effect. It is presumed that the Army Headquarters have no objection to this arrangement.

Grewal replied on 28 April 1998 as follows:

1. Col MS Jaswal, DJAG HQ 33 Corps, moved to Delhi as Staff Officer to Offg GOC-in-C Eastern Command between 05 to 07 Apr 98. Thereafter, the officer was on casual leave till 21 April 98. His presence in the Supreme Court and High Court wef 11 Apr 98 was in private capacity until he returned to HQ 33 Corps. Ex GOC 33 Corps and now GOC-in-C Eastern Command, has been cited as respondent No 4 by you in your petition. He might have taken assistance from his DJAG in his private capacity to monitor his case. **We have no intention to utilize his services for representing Union of India, COAS or the Military Secretary who have been cited by you as respondents 1 to 3.**
2 As regards utilizing services by you of DJAG HQ 1 Corps is concerned, the same yardstick would be applicable. (Emphasis added by the author).

In one of the subsequent hearings, in July 1998, when the Hon'ble Court asked for some documents pertaining to my records, it was Col MS Jaswal who had possession of my entire records and who passed these on to the court. This in fact amounted to Kalkat being given access to my confidential records. Therefore, my lawyer raised an objection. When the court asked Col MS Jaswal as to in what capacity was he handling my documents, he stated that he was representing the Union of India. This ran contrary to what the Adjutant General had conveyed to me in a written communication. The Army's JAG Maj Gen Sanan was also present in the court when this statement was made and of course did not contradict Jaswal who had actually stated a fact. It may be relevant to mention that there are sufficient number of JAG officers posted in Delhi to pursue ongoing legal cases and to represent the Union of India, and there is no need to call officers from outside Delhi for this purpose. Jaswal's statement was a factual position on the ground, and exposed the contrary view conveyed by Lt Gen Grewal in his letter dated 28 April 1998. I have mentioned this incident to highlight how as high ranking an official of the Army as the Adjutant General, could be economical with the truth. The issue did not finish there. After the DJAG of my Corps had started assisting me in my case, and was fully in picture, he was posted out to another Corps even though he had not completed his normal tenure in my Corps. This is yet another example of misuse of power.

On the point of using government resources for one's own purpose, another officer of 33 Corps – Col AS Bedi – who was actually in command of an Artillery Regiment in Sikkim, was seen in the court room during each hearing. He of course wore civil dress. Actually courtroom is an open place and there is no bar for anyone witnessing the proceedings. The only significant part was that Col Bedi moved to Delhi on temporary duty and the money was paid from official funds.

As mentioned earlier, the Government filed their Counter Affidavit (CA) in the High Court before the case came up for hearing on 20 April 1998. In this CA they repeatedly asserted that with the grant of the waiver I too had become eligible for the post of Army Commander. The government also made a strange observation in their CA. This was:

> "...It is submitted that deputation of an officer to a foreign country brings appreciable monetary gain to him, besides giving him varied exposure in a more sociable environment. It was for him to take a calculated step and decide whether he would prefer to remain in India and earn his promotions here or opt for a post on deputation in a foreign country..."

In their continued efforts to mislead the court the government were giving an impression that a person being selected and sent abroad on a posting would not be getting his promotions. They of course withheld the fact only the toppers in merit were being posted to such assignments and they all earned their due promotions subsequently. Many officers who had been Military Attaches abroad rose to become Army Chiefs (such as Gens OP Malhotra, BC Joshi) and Army Commanders (such as Lt Gens Surrinder Singh, SK Sharma, HM Khanna). Contradiction in their statement is even better understood when one recalls that even Lt Gen Kalkat had been an MA in Australia and enjoyed those 'monetary gains and social exposure'. How was it then that he was a favourite of the government and I was being singled out for discrimination?

No hearing took place in the High Court till the courts closed for summer break in 1998. These commenced only in July 1998. There were more than a dozen hearings between July and November. During these the government referred to an Army Headquarters letter dated 16 October 1992, in support of their contention that the post of an Army Commander was a selection post. Let me explain the details of this letter.

Traditionally only one name has always been sent for the post of an Army Commander or for the Director General of an Arm or Service for approval of the Appointments Committee of the Cabinet (ACC). This name has always been of the seniormost officer who has been found fit in all respects for the post, and who has the requisite residual service. In one instance the Army had similarly forwarded a single name for the post of Engineer-in-Chief. After some weeks of processing the government discovered that the officer concerned had an IB related report against him. The Army did not obviously know this input when they initiated the recommendation. When this came to light the Army was asked to recommend another name and the whole process of obtaining approval of the ACC had to be gone through again. Based on this experience the government suggested to the Army that in future it would be better that an alternate name of another officer is also sent to the government so as to save time in case the seniormost officer had something against him that may not be in the knowledge of the Army. This suggestion was only verbal and no written communication was sent on this subject. Also it had no relation to any comparison being resorted to between the two officers whose names were to be forwarded.

This Army Headquarters letter of 16 October 1992, was actually an Army Headquarters policy on the appointment of Corps Commanders. (Even the heading of the letter reads, 'Appointment of Corps Commanders') Paragraphs 7 and 8 of the letter deal with parameters for appointment of Corps Commanders are reproduced as follows:

Parameters for Appointment of Corps Commanders

7. Factors Affecting Appointment of Corps Commanders

   (a) At present there are only 11 vacancies of Corps Commanders. If we aim for a tenure of two years for Corps Commanders, the turnover per year would be between five and six: if the tenure is reduced to 18 months, the average turnover every year would be about seven.

   (b) The number of officers being cleared in the Command and Staff stream are generally larger than the number of vacancies of Corps Commanders; perforce, therefore, not all officers can be given command of a Corps, even though they may have been cleared in the Command and Staff stream.

   (c) Lt Gens are promoted according to their seniority in the promotion panels, either in a Command or Staff appointment, depending on availability. Such vacancies need not necessarily be in a Corps.

   (d) There is a Government requirement to suggest two senior eligible officers for each Army Commander's vacancy. It is, therefore, essential that when an Army commander's vacancy arises, the two seniormost officers who are eligible, in terms of the residual service rule, have completed command or are in command of a Corps.

   (e) An officer promoted to the rank of Lt Gen should be able to give viable tenures both in Command and Staff appointments.

8. *Parameters.* Taking into consideration the background and the factors affecting appointment of Corps Commanders, command of a Corps would be given, keeping the following parameters in mind:

(a) All officers who are likely to be eligible for an Army Commander's appointment, in terms of two years service, will be given command of a Corps. If such officers are promoted first on a staff vacancy, they will be given command of a Corps before their turn for consideration for Army Commander.

(b) Officers who do not have the requisite residual service/ seniority to be eligible for consideration for Army commander's appointments, may be given command of a Corps, provided they are able to give a viable tenure both in command of a Corps and in a Staff / Instructional/ERE appointment. This would normally imply that the officer has a minimum residual service of four years or more, on the date he is promoted to the rank of Lt Gen.

(c) Officers other than those covered in Para 8 (a) and (b) above, may not be given command of a Corps even though they have been cleared in the Command and Staff stream; they would instead be posted to various other staff/Instructional/ERE appointments.

During the court hearings in the High Court, the government kept harping on the out-of-context first sentence of the Para 7 (d) of the above letter and insisting that since there is a government requirement of sending two names for each Army Commander's post, it implies comparison and therefore, the Army Commander's post is a selection post. However, read in its entirety this very letter makes some points very clear. Firstly, the two names are of the seniormost officers. This leaves no doubt that seniority is in fact the main criterion other than fitness. Secondly, if comparison had to be carried out, all eligible officers of a batch have to be screened and the best chosen, as is done in all other selection boards for promotion up to the rank of Lt Gen. In my case there were a total of nine officers who were eligible for the appointment of Army Commander on 1 March 1998. Why were the other seven left out if selection was the requirement? Thirdly, the letter in Para 8 (a) makes it clear that all officers who are likely to be eligible for Army Commander's appointment in terms of the two years residual service rule, will be given command of a Corps. And how does one pick such officers? Obviously by seniority. The four years residual service rule for being appointed a Corps Commander is not applicable to these officers; it only applies to all other officers. That is why Lt Gen SK Sharma, who was late for his promotions after he returned from Germany as an MA, was given command of a Corps in 1995 even though he had less than four years residual service left. Since Sharma was senior, and since seniority is the criterion for appointment as Army Commander, he was given command of a corps irrespective of his residual service. Fourthly – this may sound ironical - from the time of issue of this letter of 16 October 1992, and till my turn came, there were 15 officers appointed as Army Commanders. All of them without exception were appointed on a single name basis because they were the seniormost officers found fit for the post. The name of the second officer was not even forwarded, leave aside carrying out any comparison. If this 16 October 1992, letter was so sacrosanct, as the government made it out, how is it that from the very time of its issue it was consistently ignored in every case till my turn came? There must indeed be some strong reason why I was singled out to the benefit of Kalkat.

There was another ground on which this 16 October 1992, letter was not accepted by the High Court. If one was to hypothetically accept that as per this letter comparison for the post of Army Commander was indeed the criterion, then virtually it overrides the government letter of 20 October 1986. How could a departmental letter issued by the MS Branch overrule a statutory letter issued in the name of the President? When this was pointed out, the government counsel insisted that this letter of 16 October 1992, too has received government approval. When the court demanded to be shown such an approval, the government could not produce it and claimed that the 'file was missing'. In the middle of the hearings the counsel was replaced by the Solicitor General to argue the government case. He of course admitted that no government approval had been obtained for this letter.

The story of my having allegedly given an 'adverse career' certificate for my Paris posting was no different. When I pointed out to the Court that I had given no such certificate and that the government had submitted a false affidavit, the government counsel kept repeating that a certificate had actually been given and kept repeating that he would produce it in the court. Finally he told the court that 'the file cannot be traced'. This, I understand, is a legal nicety amounting to accepting that no certificate exists. The government stated so many falsehoods that in its Judgment the Hon'ble Delhi High Court even mentioned it on Page 57:

> *Mr. Hegde has admitted at the bar that the revised stipulation pursuant to letter dated 16.10.1992 did not have the approval of the Ministry of Defence. As a matter of fact, respondent has taken shifting stands on said letter at the first instance, it was stated that the file was missing and when Mr. Hegde came on the scene, he fairly conceded that this additional stipulation for appointment to the post of Army commander as per letter dated 16.10.1992 was neither referred to the Ministry of Defence nor any approval there from was obtained in terms of transaction of business rules.*

During the High Court hearings it became known that they have even used against me an advisory remark that was put in one of my ACR 27 years ago when I was a Major and after which I had received all my selections and promotions in the first chance and with a unanimous verdict of the members of the Board. (The irony that even this remark was concocted and doctored while being put upto the ACC will figure later). In my writ petition and in my pleadings I had made no personal remark against Kalkat. But now I had to defend myself by filing an affidavit and pointing out that while I had received only one remark 27 years ago, and that too advisory, Kalkat had two 'adverse' remarks in his dossier; one as a Major and another in a senior rank of Colonel. The Court asked the government (since Kalkat was not pleading his case separately and his case was being fought along with the government) to file a reply. In this reply they admitted that the remarks did exist but pleaded that the alleged remarks are not adverse in nature. Even if, for the sake of argument, one was to accept that the remarks in Kalkat's record were not adverse and were only advisory, the question arises as to why were these not highlighted in his career profile in the same manner as my only advisory remark was highlighted? It is obvious that the concocted comparison was only to support a pre-determined decision and not to decide who was better through a fair evaluation.

During the course of the hearings even Gen VP Malik gave an affidavit. It read:

I, General V.P. Malik, PVSM, AVSM, ADC, Chief of the Army Staff, South Block, New Delhi do hereby solemnly affirm and declare as under:

1. *That I am the Chief of the Army Staff since 01 October 1997.*
2. *That on 28th February 1998, Lt Gen Ravi Eipe, General Officer Commanding-in-Chief (GOC-in-C) Eastern Command retired and on 2nd March 1998, I forwarded a proposal for the appointment of GOC-in-C, Eastern Command.*

3. *That as per the existing guidelines, I considered the petitioner and Respondent No. 4 for appointment to the post of GOC-in-C, Eastern Command and having carefully considered the matter in its entirety, I found Respondent No. 4 to be more suitable for the said appointment and accordingly, I recommended the name of Respondent No. 4 for the said appointment and gave my reasons for that, to the Ministry of Defence for consideration by the appointing authority.*
4. *That my recommendations were bonafide, in good faith and in the best interest of Army and I never had any illwill, bias or prejudice against the petitioner and had no extraneous reasons or considerations in my mind while recommending the name of Respondent No. 4. I had also forwarded the career profile of the petitioner alongwith that of Respondent No. 4 for consideration by the Competent authority.*
5. *That the Annual Confidential Report for the year 1997-98 alone could not be made the basis of appointment of the petitioner to the post of GOC-in-C, Eastern Command and while recommending the overall profile of the two senior most eligible officers and recommended the more suitable person.*

Deponent

Verification

I, the above named deponent, do hereby verify that contents of the above affidavit are true and correct to my knowledge and belief and that nothing material has been concealed therefrom.

Verified on the 17th Day of July 1998.

(Deponenet)

To understand whether Gen Malik gave a truthful affidavit or not, it is important to recount a few other related facts.

The only government letter for appointment of Army Commander is the one dated 20 October 1986 (and its amendment issued vide letter dated 18 November 1996.) Other than these there are no government instructions, guidelines or orders on the subject. These two letters clearly indicate that the appointment is to be based on fitness and residual service. That Gen VP Malik was fully aware of the rule position of the Army Commander's post being filled by the seniormost eligible officer, is not in doubt. As brought out earlier, when his own chance of becoming an Army Commander suddenly occurred due to the demise of Gen BC Joshi, he wrote a letter on 24 November 1994, to the newly appointed COAS, Gen Shankar Roychowdhury, where he clearly indicated knowledge of the rule position. Besides, at the time of filing the affidavit Gen Malik could not have been unaware that when he was actually appointed Army Commander in 1995, no other name was included in the proposal. The proposal sent by the then COAS on 04 April 1995, had read as under:

> *A statement showing the eligibility of the General Officers in order of their seniority, up to the point of retirement of Lt. Gen Surinder Nath, PVSM, AVSM, ADC, VCOAS is placed opposite. It will be seen from the statement that Lt. Gen VP Malik, AVSM, Commandant Defence Services Staff College Wellington will be the senior most eligible General Officer for the Army Commander's appointment on 01 Jul 95 in terms of two years residual service. Since Lt Gen VP Malik, AVSM has earned clear recommendations for promotion as Army Commander/ VCOAS and has an Above Average career profile, I am of the opinion that there is no need to analyse*

career profiles of other officers junior to him and are eligible for consideration for the appointment of Army Commander/VCOAS in terms of residual service.

The proposal further confirms that seniority and residual service are the only conditions for the appointment of Army Commander. Compare the above to my own career profile put up to the ACC by (I guess) Gen Malik himself on 2 Mar 1998. It read:

...The overall profile of the officer especially in senior ranks has been clearly above average. All the reporting officers gave him above average ratings with sprinkling of outstanding ratings.

It would be clear that Gen Malik has applied a different yardstick in my case compared to his own case. The instructions that existed in 1995 continued to remain in force also in 1998. Therefore, when Gen Malik says in his affidavit, 'That as per the existing guidelines, I considered the petitioner and Respondent No. 4...' he makes a false statement because there are no other existing guidelines for comparing two names.

I had been promoted from Maj Gen to Lt Gen by the selection board held in April 1997. The selection board had taken into consideration my overall profile. The very fact that I was found fit and promoted is proof in itself that my overall profile was without blemish. Gen Malik had also examined my overall career profile while recommending my statutory complaint for a waiver on 6 January 1998. (Reader may recollect he had stated '...examined the same against his overall profile and other relevant documents...') The only new addition to that profile was my CR in the rank of Lt Gen. In the normal course, this ACR for the year 1997-98 was to be written on 1 July 1998. However, the Army asked for a special report covering period up to 31 January 1998. The IO wrote it on 08 February 1998, and by the SRO (who was the COAS,

Gen Malik himself) on 27 February 1998. The sole purpose of this report was to assess my fitness for the post of Army Commander. That is why the COAS delayed sending his recommendation for the appointment of Army Commander till after this report was written. If this report was not to have any bearing then where was the need to wait for it? The only reason why the Army Chief waited for my report to be written was that this was the only additional input required for deciding on the appointment of Army Commander.

In the past the only three Lt Generals ever to have been denied the post of Army Commander (Maya Dass, IJ Khanna and GL Bakshi), were so denied only because of negative recommendations in their ACR as Corps Commanders, though they had a good overall profile. The ACR as the Corps Commander is thus the only instrument to decide one's fitness as Army Commander; the overall profile of course is there but it has already been considered at the time of one's promotion to the rank of Lt Gen. When Gen Malik wrote my ACR on 27 February 1998, he had my entire career profile available to him and when he found me fit for promotion it was keeping in mind my overall profile.

Even at the time the then Lt Gen Malik's case was recommended by Gen Shankar Roychowdhury, the recommendation had said, *'It will be seen from the statement that Lt. Gen VP Malik, AVSM, Commandant Defence Services Staff College Wellington will be the senior most eligible General Officer for the Army Commander's appointment on 01 Jul 95 in terms of two years residual service. Since Lt Gen VP Malik, AVSM has earned clear recommendations for promotion as Army Commander/VCOAS and has an Above Average career profile ...'* This leaves no doubt that apart from overall profile, the report earned as an Lt Gen, which includes recommendations for next higher rank and appointment, is the clinching/deciding factor. How was my case different from Malik's own? We were both seniormost eligible General officers for the Army Commander's appointment in terms of the two-year residual service; we both had earned clear recommendations for promotion as Army commander/VCOAS; and we both had an overall above average career profile (in fact I had a sprinkling of outstanding reports that he did not have). When Gen Malik said in his affidavit, *'That the Annual Confidential Report for the year 1997-98 alone could not be made the basis of appointment of the petitioner to the post of GOC-in-C'*, **he seemed to imply and convey to the Hon'ble court that apart from the overall profile and the report as Lt Gen, there was some other factor that was against me and in favour of Kalkat. What that hidden factor was has never been made clear to me by any one, either directly or through the courts.**

Interestingly, in his affidavit, Gen Malik introduced a new factor by stating that he found Kalkat *more suitable* for the post. The term 'suitability' is not found in any of the government letters while talking of the appointment of an Army Commander. Nor has it ever been taken into consideration in the past, or even in case of all the Army Commanders appointed after my case. Suitability is a subjective term and varies with different individuals making assessment on someone. Gen Malik had to take recourse to such terminology to try to find some justification for his otherwise unjustifiable recommendation.

Gen Malik also falsely stated in his affidavit that *'nothing material has been concealed therefrom'*. He concealed from the ACC the fact that Kalkat had two adverse entries in his ACRs. Considering the fact that the only advisory remark in one of my reports that was written over 27 years ago was included in my profile, it was material that Kalkat's adverse remarks were also included, if the two profiles were to be fairly compared.

Gen Malik also makes another false statement in Para 5 of his affidavit when he says, '...*while recommending the overall profile of the two senior most eligible officers...*' On 02 March 1998, when he initiated the recommendation, I did not have the waiver from minimum one-year command of a Corps; that was given only on 16 March 1998. Therefore, technically, I was not eligible when he sent his recommendation. In actual fact therefore, he sent only one name of eligible Lt Gen (that of Kalkat). Logically he should have withheld sending recommendation till disposal by the government of my statutory complaint that he had himself recommended on 06 January 1998. On 02 March 1998, even if he had recommended my name for the post, the ministry would have returned it on the grounds of my ineligibility. Or else, if two names were indeed required to be sent for comparison as they repeatedly claimed during the court hearings, Malik should have sent names of Kalkat and the Lt Gen next in seniority that was eligible. The way the recommendation was initiated, it is difficult to avoid the inference that there was a pre-determined decision to appoint Kalkat.

Gen Malik had to give the affidavit out of legal compulsion. His falsehoods are apparently to cover a vital mystery. On Friday 27 February 1998, when he wrote my report after witnessing my war game, and when my overall career profile was available to him, he found me fit for the post of Army Commander. Barely two days later, on 2 March 1998, when he sent the recommendations to the government, he changed his mind. Everything else was to cover up that sudden mysterious change. **Something must have happened over that weekend!**

The High Court Judgment

The Delhi High Court announced its judgment on 11 December 1998. It is a very detailed judgment running into

64 pages in which the Court quashed the appointment of Lt Gen Kalkat as Army Commander Eastern Command. Since the government had been making contradictory statements, the Hon'ble Court called for government files and quoted extensively from these in the judgment. The operative part of the judgment is reproduced below:

Mr. Hegde also contended that the change in the policy pursuant to the letter of 16.10.1992 was not illegal and even the departmental instructions providing certain yard-sticks and criterion in addition to what was provided in 1986 is applicable to the petitioner. In his contentions, he has sited the case of Lt. Genl. R.K. Anand Vs. Union of India & anr. AIR 1992 SC 763. The authority cited by the respondent i.e. Lt. Genl. R.K. Anand Vs. Union of India & anr. (supra) is also of no help to the respondent as Mr. Hegde has admitted at the bar that the revised stipulation pursuant to letter dated 16.10.1992 did not have the approval of the Ministry of Defence. As a matter of fact, respondent has taken shifting stands on said letter at the first instance, it was stated that file was missing and when Mr. Hegde came on the scene, he fairly conceded that this additional stipulation for appointment to the post of Army Commander as per letter dated 16.10.1992 was neither referred to the Ministry of Defence nor any approval therefrom was obtained in terms of transaction of business rules. Even in Lt. Genl. R.K.Anand Vs. Union of India & anr's case (supra) the Court did not quash the policy as it came to the conclusion that the communication therein dated 9 September 1986, had received the concurrence of the concerned Ministry. It was held:

> *".........we inspected the department file and found that the matter was referred to the Ministry of Defence and had received the approval of the Prime Minister. In view of the same it is not possible to accede to the*

> *submission of the appellant that the letter of 9th September, 1986 is merely a departmental communication and cannot be raised to the pedestal of an exclusive instruction under Art. 162 Of the Constitution........."*

In the instant case, in view of the fact that no such concurrence was received from the Ministry of Defence nor circular/letter dated 16.10.1992 has been agreed re-defining the parameters for promotion to the post of Army Commander, it can be said that it was a policy decision adversely affecting the rights of the petitioner. It will be germane to the controversy that even the note of the Cabinet Secretary as well as of the Ministry regarding the parameters for promotion to the post of Army Commander has not mentioned the additional clause of sending names of two senior eligible officers in terms of 16.10 1992, therefore, it can be safely said that same has not been taken into consideration at all.

The only question before me is whether post of Army Commander which became available on 1.3.1998 on the retirement of Lt. General Ravi Eipe wherein the petitioner and respondent No. 4 were considered whether the appointment of respondent No. 4 as Army Commander in spite of petitioner being admittedly senior to respondent No. 4 was justified. The argument advanced by the respondent that Circular dated 16.10.1992 was complementary to the Circular dated 20.10.1986 does not inspire any confidence. As I have already stated that that letter neither had the approval of the Ministry of Defence nor was ever put before Ministry in terms of transaction of business rules and by no stretch of imagination, it can be said that it was issued under Article 73 of the Constitution. This purported clause, which has been introduced vide letter dated 16.10.1992, even does not find mention in the note of the Cabinet Secretary sent to the Prime Minister for appointment to the post of Army

Commander wherein the petitioner and respondent No. 4 were considered.

The public interest is best secured when reasonable opportunities for promotion exist for all qualified employees, when superior civil servants are enabled to move up as rapidly the promotion ladder under the said rules, which in the present case is seniority-cum-fitness and as vacancies occur and the selection is made on the basis of known criterion. It eliminates favouritism and the system is transparent so as to infuse confidence among all the ranks in the army, and is devoid of suspicion. The whole rationale of the principle of seniority-cum-fitness is that seniority should determine the order in which an officer of a particular grade should be considered for promotion. Those considered unfit may be passed over. This means that the seniority-cum-fitness principle and what it implies is that the senior person unless unfit should get the promotion automatically. Under this principle seniority ought to have been given preponderating weight.

Thus, it is seen that the appointment of Army Commander is a selection grade appointment to be filled from eligible corps commander or those who have commanded corps. Prior to 1986 Corps commanders subject to positive recommendation in their C.Rs. became Army Commanders. In 1986 a criteria of two years residual service was introduced for their becoming Army Commanders subject to their being found fit in every respect. General officers meeting the said criteria were promoted in the order of their seniority. Seniority was ignored in the case of non-recommendation in the C.Rs. One year command of a Corps was added to the criteria prescribed in 1986 letter vide November 1996 letter which also stipulated waiver by the competent authority. Any other criterion for such appointment would amount to hostile discrimination which would be violative of Articles 14 and 16 of the Constitution of India. As I have discussed earlier the letter dated 16.10.1992 of the Army Headquarters cannot be invoked in the aid of respondent as the same is not statutory in nature. I find considerable force from the perusal of the files of the respondents that prior to October, 1992 senior most eligible officers were always appointed as Army Commanders if he was otherwise fit. After the petitioner was found suitable for appointment as Army Commander and graded fit for promotion in terms of the C.Rs. of the petitioner and the requirement of minimum merit having been met the petitioner ought to have been promoted on the basis of admitted seniority. The ACR form for Lt General does not contain numerical grading which is the case up to the rank of Major General. The evaluation of the rating in the ACR of the Lt General is indicated by simple 'Yes' or 'No' in respect of an officer's fitness for next promotion on the basis of the proforma, there is no scope for argument that comparative merit among eligible officers is a yardstick for promotion to the post of Army commander. The criteria for promotion to the rank of Army commander is thus based on the criteria laid down in the Defence Ministry's letters dated 20.10.1986 and 18.11.1996. Even if the perusal of the record of the respondent and seeing the career profiles of the petitioner and respondent No. 4 both being eligible, fit and equal in merit, it cannot be said that petitioner could have been superseded in view of respondent No. 4's longer tenure as corps commander as length of tenure as corps commander was not a laid down criteria in terms of the criteria stipulated in the letter of 20.10.1986 and 18.11.1996 for promotion to the post of Army Commander. The note of the Cabinet Secretary in which he has comparatively discussed the ACRs of 1971 of the petitioner amounts to importing a non-existence criteria after the petitioner was found fit in all respects in the ACR on the basis of which he was to be promoted to the next higher rank. The minimum tenure of one year as Corps Commander in terms of letter of the Government of India dated 18.11.1996 has also been met by the petitioner on account of the grant of waiver by the Government. From the perusal of the files of the respondent, I find force in the arguments of the petitioner that the delay in the decision on the statutory complaint submitted by the petitioner on 5.10.1997 also created hindrance for his next promotion. The post of the Army Commander fell vacant on 1.3.1998 and the statutory complaint of the petitioner was decided on 16.3.1998. There is considerable force in the arguments of the learned counsel for the petitioner that the prayer to seek review the 'deferment' grading awarded by the selection board held on 31.10.1996, respondent rejected the prayer vide their letter dated 16.3.1998 on the pretext that the petitioner must have furnished adverse career certificate. From the files of the respondent it is not found that how a note was put up that petitioner has given willingness certificate as no such certificate was produced by the respondent. I think this mistake was committed on account of a note written by the Joint Secretary on supposition that the petitioner might have submitted an adverse career certificate.

(Author's Note: The Hon'ble Court has been rather magnanimous in letting off the concerned Joint Secretary, Mr. Akhil K. Jain. How can a Government of India letter be issued based on a supposition? The entire records are available to the dealing bureaucrats while drafting/issuing such documents. Either I had given a willingness certificate, in which case it is there in the records or it was simply not given and it is not there. There is no such thing as 'might have submitted'. It is highly unlikely that a senior officer of the Ministry of Defence would commit an error of this nature. The truth may be different. The government had no administrative, legal or any other ground to change my grading from 'fit' to 'deferred' in the 31 October 1996 selection board. Therefore, they had no ground to reject my main prayer of reviewing this action of theirs. If they accept my prayer then I become an Lt Gen and a Corps commander retrospectively thus thwarting their design through issue of new policy dated 18 November 1996 of minimum one year command of a Corps. The only way they could find an excuse to reject my main prayer was through this charade of a 'supposed mistake'. Such is the arbitrariness that is exercised by those in charge of dealing with the career prospects of senior Army officers.)

One thing surprised this Court that the way the respondent filed the counter affidavit submitting therein that the Lt. General IJ Khanna, Maya Dass and GL Bakshi though senior most were overlooked on the basis of comparative merit. From the perusal of files of these officers it is manifestly clear that those officers were overlooked on account of their C.Rs. as Corps commanders, therefore, they did not fulfill the fitness criteria and were not eligible for promotion to the post of Army Commander. (Author's Note: This falsehood was first stated by Gen VP Malik in his note to the Defence Ministry on 06 March 1998.)

Thus, I hold that the 'deferment' grading in October'1996 of the selection board has also adversely affected the petitioner. It has direct bearing on his exposure to command a Corps. The letter dated 18.11.1996 laying down that henceforth an officer to become eligible to be an Army Commander, should have commanded a Corps for at least one year and its applicability from the date of issue unlike in the past when the letter which was issued in the year 1986 was made operative in 1988 has only affected the petitioner as has been discussed by me in detail in the preceding paragraphs.

For the reasons stated above, I have no hesitation in quashing the appointment of respondent No. 4 as Army Commander, Eastern Command. I, therefore, allow the writ petition and quash the appointment of respondent No. 4 as

Army Commander, Eastern Command. A writ of mandamus is also issued to the respondents to appoint the petitioner as Army Commander forthwith as he is admittedly the senior most Lt. General in the Army and has been found fit in terms of his A.C.R. Rule is made absolute.

There will be no order as to costs.

The government immediately went into an appeal challenging the judgment. The Delhi High Court Bench heard the appeal on 16 December 1998. The government plea was dismissed on the spot. The brief order dictated by the Hon'ble Bench in the court itself read as follows:

> *The circular dated October 20, 1986 by virtue of which the President of India laid down criteria for the appointment of Army Commander/Vice Chief of Army Staff inter alia stipulates that "The officer should be fit in every respect for such appointment". It is, therefore, evident that comparative merit of officers is neither the requirement nor is it permissible. What is not permissible has in fact been done by the appellants. They have compared the record of the senior most officer, namely, the writ petitioner with the officer below him, namely, Lt. General H.R.S. Kalkat. The appellants have treated the post of Army Commander as a selection post. We are in agreement with the opinion of the learned Single Judge that it is not a selection post. It would have been a different matter, if the senior most officer had been found not to be fit in every respect and in that eventuality, the authorities would have considered the next senior officer who may be eligible. However, that is not so. The writ petitioner was not held to be unfit in terms of the circular dated 20th October, 1986 and instead the post was treated as selection post and comparative merit of the two officers adjudged which*

is wholly unwarranted in law as rightly held by learned Single Judge. We are also in agreement with the opinion of the learned Single Judge that in the past too, single person was considered and if not found fit then alone the next in seniority was considered. The reliance of the Government on the circular dated 16th October, 1992 has been rightly rejected by learned Single Judge. It is a non-statutory document. It does not have the approval of the President/Government of India. The decision in the case State Bank of India & Ors. Vs. Mohd. Mynuddin, (1987) 4 SCC 486 relied upon by Mr. Santosh Hegde, learned Solicitor General has no applicability. That was a case where a selection post was under consideration. The observations made by the supreme Court in State of Mysore Vs. C.R. Sheshadri & Ors., (1974) 4 SCC 308 have been diluted in B.V. Sivaiah & Ors. Vs. K. Addanki Babu & Ors., 1984 (4) SCALE 182. Rather it has been held that the observations in Sheshadri's case cannot be regarded as correctly reflecting as to what is meant by the criteria of 'seniority-cum-merit'. In the present case, the criteria is not even seniority-cum-merit. It is seniority-cum-fitness which in other words means seniority subject to rejection of unfit. We find no infirmity in the view taken by learned Single Judge. The appeal is accordingly dismissed. Dasti

I would like to place on record my deep appreciation for the senior advocate Mr. RK Anand who represented me in the High Court. It took more than a dozen hearings. Mr. Anand is a well-known name in legal and political circles and I can hardly say anything to add to his professional credentials. But I would certainly like to mention about his personal magnanimity and kind-heartedness. Our contact started totally on a professional note. As time passed we struck u p a personal rapport that has resulted into a lasting friendship which I shall always cherish.

7

A Question of Ethics

I had been warned by well wishers that the Army Chief would not let any opportunity pass where he could catch me in some other case. Apart from drawing attention away from the ongoing court case, and his falsehoods that were being exposed, it would also 'fix' me for good. That attempt came in 1999.

During Operation Vijay I was deployed along the western front with my Corps. The Army Commander, Lt Gen Surjit Singh Sangra, came on a routine visit. After the usual discussion on operational matters he asked to see me alone. The other officers were accordingly asked to leave. He informed me that he had received a communication from Gen Malik alleging that while the Army was fighting the Kargil war I was holidaying with my family in Leh (Ladakh). He further added that Gen Malik had termed my action/behaviour as unethical.

I was quite surprised at this false accusation. I told the Army Commander that I had last visited Ladakh on official duty in June 1998 where, as Colonel of the Rajputana Rifles Regiment, I had gone to meet one of the battalions on the eve of their induction into the Glaciers. This was much before the Kargil War. I had spent two days in the Battalion location far away from Leh, and that I had gone alone without any member of the family. Lt Gen Sangra merely repeated what the Army Chief had communicated to him. However, during further discussion it transpired that on the alleged dates of my 'holiday', Lt Gen Sangra himself had visited one of my Divisions on the western front and I happened to be there. This alibi seemingly ended the matter, or at least I heard nothing further on the subject.

I learnt later that the Army Chief had possibly received his information (about my alleged holidaying) from the intelligence sources. The Army Chief has the entire Army resources at his disposal. Which agency is to be utilised for what purpose is solely a matter of his discretion. I have therefore no comment on the fact that the intelligence agencies were being used for tailing inconvenient Generals of the Army. However, I cannot resist stating an obvious fact, even though it is somewhat out of context for this narrative. If the Army Chief had utilised his intelligence agencies for their more legitimate task of gaining intelligence from across the border, may be we could have avoided the national shame of Kargil and would have saved some of the precious lives that were lost in pushing back the aggressor.

What hurt me more in the entire episode was the reported adverse comment by Gen Malik on my ethical standards. I can say with pride that throughout my service in uniform I had followed the highest ethical norms and standards. I take strong exception to anyone casting aspersions on my ethical values, least of all a persona like Gen VP Malik. I would like to elaborate on this and apprise the reader why I am taking Gen Malik's name in particular.

I have already highlighted in an earlier chapter the letter the then Lt Gen VP Malik wrote to the newly appointed Army Chief, Gen Shankar Roychowdhury, on 24 November 1994, in connection with his claim to be appointed an Army Commander. In this communication, having conceded that with the first two vacancies going to his two batchmates but his seniors, and that he would thus miss out on the chance of becoming an Army Commander, he raised another point concerning one of these two officers i.e. Lt Gen KL D'Souza. While adding a sweetener that he wished Kevin (Lt Gen KL D'Souza) well, etc, he said that he had learnt that Lt Gen D'Souza was in low medical category and that efforts were being made to review his low category. He told the Army Chief that that it would be technically wrong to keep a vacancy unfilled awaiting Kevin to get medically upgraded. He questioned this keeping in mind, as he said, ethics and norms. The fact is that an officer's medical papers are personal and confidential documents. For the then Lt Gen Malik, located far away in Wellington, methods adopted in 'acquiring' that information (of efforts being made to review D'Souza's medical category) in those six days, could not have been based entirely on ethical means. How it was possibly done had been a hot gossip topic in the Army circles at that time.

It is nobody's case that a medically unfit person should be appointed Army Commander. However, there is a system in place and the medical authorities are very fair and strict in applying standards of medical fitness. They themselves would have taken care of this aspect. Malik, in raising this point with the Army Chief, was entirely inspired by his personal ambition. Instead of questioning the ethics and norms of the Army, if anything it was Malik's action to do down a colleague that could be termed 'unethical'. Besides, it also showed his lack of faith in the system.

One should certainly fight for one's rights. But it is for the reader to assess whether it is ethical to do down a colleague in the process of trying to rise in the hierarchy. In the case of Gen Malik it was even more ironical, because after he became the Army Chief, he never tired of laying stress on the 'buddy system' in the Army, a concept he did not himself appear to have followed in practice.

Let me give another example of Gen Malik's ethical standards. He took over as the Southern Army Commander on 1 July 1995, being the seniormost eligible Lt Gen at the time. It was now known that on the date of retirement of Gen Shankar Roychowdhury on 30 September 1997, VP Malik would be the seniormost serving Army Commander and would be due to be appointed the Army Chief. The line was clear, based on his seniority.

A small hurdle came in 1996. The government began to consider two years extension for all government employees, including the Army. As per procedure in the Army, at every level views are sought from the next below rung in the hierarchy right down to the lowest unit. This system ensures that the opinion of a cross section of the entire Army down to the soldiers gets woven into the final decision. The views are then forwarded in the reverse, to one-up headquarters in the chain and these are then compiled at the highest level at Army Headquarters for further submission to the government. Therefore, on the subject of the proposed extension of retirement age by two years, the Army Headquarters sought views from all the Commands.

When the views were compiled at the Army Headquarters every single Regional Command as well as the Army Training Command had given views in favour of the extension. The only Command opposing the proposal was the Southern

Command, headed by Lt Gen VP Malik. The ostensible reason given was that extension would raise the age of serving personnel across the board and run contrary to the youthful profile of the Army. It is unlikely that soldiers serving in the jurisdiction of Southern Command would have had a perception different from the rest of their colleagues in the entire Army. It appears the difference in perception was only in the thinking of Lt Gen Malik individually. And there was a reason. If this extension had come about in 1996, then Lt Gen SK Sharma, being senior would have become the Army Chief instead of Malik.

The extension did not come in 1996 and, based on his seniority, VP Malik became the Army Chief on 1 October 1997. In the normal course he would have held the post till 31 October 1999, when he would have retired on reaching the age of 60 years as per rules in force.

The subject of extension resurfaced in 1998. Again the government sought views from all the organisations, including the Army. This time Gen Malik calculated that he would personally gain by the extension, in that, he would get to serve as the Army Chief up to 30 September 2000, i.e. for a period of three years tenure. This would thus give him an additional 11 months in the Chief's chair. Based on this calculation this time his recommendation was in favour of the extension. The need for Army's youthful profile was given a clean go by. On both occasions Gen VP Malik's recommendations appear to have been driven by his personal ambition and not by the genuine interests of Army as an organisation. I wonder if his actions could be termed ethical.

The High Court judgement reproduced a copy of my profile that was put up to the Prime Minister. The profile was greatly falsified and coloured to do me down and to show Kalkat in a better light in comparison. (The details would figure later). The profile presumably was prepared by the Army and would have gone to the Ministry through the Army Chief along with his recommendations. Was it ethical to falsify my record to bring Kalkat in a better light? Let the reader make his own judgment.

It is public knowledge that even after being informed of the Kargil intrusion on 15 May 1999 (Saturday), Gen VP Malik, instead of rushing back, chose to continue his foreign trip and returned only on 20 May 1999. Let the reader judge the ethicality of this.

All I wish to state is that a person who himself placed his own personal interests above the interests of the Army and the country, should have no moral right to cast aspersions on the ethical standards of others.

8

The Case in Supreme Court

After losing at two successive levels, as expected, the government filed an SLP in the Supreme Court on 17 December 1998. The case was to come up in the Supreme Court next day. On 17 December the Judge Advocate's Department of the Army organized their annual dinner. Actually, this dinner was scheduled for a later date but was advanced to 17 December at a short notice, to suit the convenience of Hon'ble members of the judiciary as the courts were closing on 18 December for winter. On this occasion the Hon'ble members of the judiciary were also invited. Mr. RK Anand, the senior advocate who had fought my case in the Delhi High Court, also attended the dinner as an invitee and narrated an interesting incident to me the next day.

Mr. Anand had known Gen VP Malik, the Chief of the Army Staff. When they met at the dinner gathering, Gen Malik started talking about my case where the Delhi Court Bench had delivered a judgment in my favour the previous day. At that time, Dr AS Anand, the Hon'ble Chief Justice of India, also joined the gathering and met the Army Chief. Gen

Malik remarked to the Hon'ble Chief Justice that Mr. RK Anand was troubling the Army in my matter. To this Mr. RK Anand replied, "when the Army is right, I appear for them; but when they are wrong, the Army is at the receiving end".

I have two valid comments on this incident. Firstly, was it proper or ethical for the Army Chief to speak about my case to the Chief Justice of India, before whose Bench the case was to be heard the next morning? The second comment touches a much larger issue. As an organization, the Army has the largest number of cases in progress before the courts, and is thus the judiciary's biggest defending litigant. Therefore, it is debatable whether the Hon'ble members of the judiciary should accept hospitality of the Army. It may not influence their judgments. But it creates the possibility of raising doubts in the minds of petitioners who are fighting cases against the government. This goes against the basic principle that says 'justice must not only be done but must also be seen to be done.'

Two SLPs were filed in the Supreme Court challenging the judgment of the High Court. One, expectedly, was filed by the Union of India. The second SLP was filed by Lt Gen Kalkat, in which he made the Government of India also a respondent. Interestingly, throughout the hearings in the High Court, Kalkat had not engaged a separate lawyer, nor had he filed a separate reply. He was fighting the case as part of the Government of India. It appears to be irregular, almost unheard of, that person who chose not to defend himself in the High Court, is allowed to file a separate petition in the Supreme Court. Focus of Kalkat's SLP now was on questioning my eligibility in terms of the requirement of command of a Corps for a period of one year. The Government of India could not have done this since they had made me eligible after the grant of six months' waiver in the command of a Corps. It also appears irregular that new facts are allowed to be introduced at the Supreme Court level. We objected to Kalkat filing an SLP and bringing in the new fact of my eligibility. The apex court overruled us.

Kalkat's SLP was full of falsehoods; he had even framed his own criteria for appointment of Army Commanders which is not provided for in the government orders. The reader can judge whether it was an effort by Kalkat in his individual capacity or it was in connivance with the government, by perusing the following.

One of the points mentioned by Kalkat in his SLP was... 'It is submitted that the then Raksha Mantri (Shri Mulayam Singh Yadav) signed the file on 15.03.1998 (last day in the office) approving grant of six months waiver to the Respondent No 1 while deciding his Statutory Complaint, even though there could have been a difference of opinion between the Army Headquarters, and the Ministry of Defence functionaries upto the level of Defence secretary...'

It is not my contention to comment on the moral righteousness or wrongness for a minister to sign files on the last day in office. The point I am making is that the person who drafted the SLP had clear access to the government files and the details of which bureaucrat gave what opinion on the file. Such confidential information being made available to a petitioner, who has made the Union of India a respondent, is indeed strange. Or was it drafted by the government functionaries who found it convenient to have their decision (of granting waiver) questioned through enactment of this charade?

Kalkat's effort was apparently to create an impression that Shri Mulayam Singh Yadav had done me a special favour by granting the waiver, even though it was redundant on the date it was granted. It was ironical because it was during the regime of Shri Mulayam Singh himself that the initial damage was done to me when, apparently in order to promote and accommodate Maj Gen BS Malik, my grading was changed from 'fit' to 'deferred' in the 31 October 1996 Selection Board. Also, it was during the same regime that the new stipulation of minimum command of a Corps for one year was introduced without any lead-time and knowing that it would adversely affect only me. Also, it was during that very regime that my 'deferred' grading, though approved by the ACC on 29 November 1996, was not disclosed till March 1997 thus effectively preventing the Army from convening another selection board in the interim period. Additionally, the delay in disposing of my statutory complaint till well past the date of vacancy of an Army Commander's post and when the recommendations involving my super session had already been made, had occurred under the same very regime.

The above content of the SLP raises another pertinent question. Why were the **Ministry of Defence functionaries up to the level of Defence Secretary so keen to go against the recommendations of the Army Chief?**

The government SLP was first heard in the Court on 18 December 1998. In that hearing the court stayed the operation of the High Court order where the conditional appointment of Lt Gen Kalkat had been quashed. The order of the Court dated 18.12.1998 was:

Coram: Hon'ble the Chief Justice
Hon'ble Mr Justice VN Khare
Hon'ble Mr Justice MB Shah

Order

"Till the matters are listed before the Motion Bench in the month of January, 1999, the operation of the impugned judgments shall stay".

The next hearing took place on 21 January 1999. During this hearing the Hon'ble Court observed that the matter involving senior posts in the Army was sensitive in nature and should not be heard in the court. They wanted a solution to be found outside the court just as the Hon'ble Court pointed out, the government had done in another case involving an Air Force officer. The court expressed happiness that the concerned Air Force officer had been promoted without the case being heard in the court. The court advised my lawyer, Mr PP Rao, to submit a proposal to the Attorney General. I asked myself whether the two contesting parties (that is, Union of India and I) were being treated equal in the eyes of the law; because if that were so, the proposal – which in fact amounted to a compromise - should have been asked for from the government since they had lost the case at two successive levels.

The Court further directed that we should come back to them in eight weeks. When the Court mentioned the period of eight weeks, my lawyer pointed out that it was too long. The Hon'ble Court then remarked that in case we were ready earlier, we could approach the Court accordingly. On being further asked whether this would require an application being filed by us, the Court told my lawyer that there was no need for an application, remarking, "*we are sitting here only, you can approach us any time.*"

The court hearing of 21 January 1999, ended giving following orders:

Coram: Hon'ble the Chief Justice
Hon'ble Mr Justice M Srinivasan
Hon'ble Justice UC Banerjee

Order:

"SLP (C) Nos. 20511-20512/98

Leave granted.

Printing dispensed with. The appeal shall be heard on the SLP paper books. Additional documents, if any, may be filed within eight weeks.

The interim direction shall continue to operate in the meanwhile.

The matters require expeditious disposal. Liberty to mention..."

As directed by the Court my lawyer on my behalf gave the proposal to the Attorney General. A copy is reproduced here:

To
The Attorney General of India
New Delhi

Proposal on Behalf of Respondent no 1 in the Matter of Union of India & ORS Vs Lt Gen R S Kadyan and ANR Civil Appeal no. 359-360 oF 1999

Sir,

1. *Pursuant to the suggestion of the Hon'ble Supreme Court, the following proposal is made.*
2. *The Appeals can be disposed of by the Hon'ble Supreme Court without expressing any opinion on the merits if the Govt appoints Respondent No 1 (Lt Gen RS Kadyan) with effect from the same date on which Respondent No 2 (Lt Gen HRS Kalkat) was appointed as Army Commander (20.4.1998), with all consequential reliefs by creating a suitable post of Army Commander so as not to affect his (Respondent No 1) eligibility for consideration for further promotion on the basis of the said retrospective appointment.*

3 Feb 1999
(Rajiv Dutta)
Advocate Supreme Court of India

There is an unfortunate misconception in the minds of some officers (who are not familiar with details) that I was insisting on taking over only Eastern Command or that I was keen only to bring down Kalkat. As would be seen from the above proposal given to the Attorney General, I had not insisted or even suggested that Kalkat be brought down from his conditional appointment. I had merely suggested that I be appointed from the same date as he was appointed. This would have been possible through creation of another post of Army Commander. This would have ensured that our relative seniority was maintained while at the same time not disturbing Kalkat from the post.

There was no response from the Attorney General of any kind to our proposal. After eight weeks had come and gone without any progress, we had no choice but to approach the Court again. This was done through 'mentioning', as had been permitted by the Court. The matter came up before the Bench of the Hon'ble Chief Justice on 16 April 1999. Although it was over twelve weeks after the last court hearing on 21 January 1999, whereas the court had wanted the matter to be heard after eight weeks (or earlier if we were ready), to our surprise the Hon'ble Bench headed by the CJI expressed annoyance and verbally observed that since we were putting pressure on them, they would list the matter in January 2001. The Advocate of course apologised to the Hon'ble Bench. Thereafter, the court issued the following order:

Let the appeals be processed for early hearing".

To me as a non-legal person, this development appeared strange. We were after all only following the orders of the Hon'ble Court itself. The only possible reason, that I could analyse, was that the Hon'ble Bench (headed by the Chief Justice) must have been overly busy with more important cases and our seeming insistence irritated them. I, therefore, suggested to my legal advisors that I wished to file an application requesting a change of Bench. This fetched a howl of protest from the experts. While conceding that legally I could do so, they opined that if I followed this course, two outcomes would be inevitable as this would tantamount to showing lack of faith in the Hon'ble Chief Justice himself. First, no lawyer would fight my case. Second, it would cause prejudice to any other bench where the matter was listed. Being a very sensitive issue I dropped it, albeit with reluctance. I still had a faint hope that the final hearing may still come before a different Bench in the normal course.

The Government however, refused to create another vacancy that could have accommodated both Kalkat and me without disturbing our inter se seniority and without taking away the rightful due of anyone down the ladder coming up for the post after us. It may be mentioned that such creation of additional post at the level of an Army Commander/Vice Chief was not without precedent. At one time during 1985, the Army had three Vice Chiefs of Army Staff as against the one authorised post. My suggestion for creation of additional post of Army Commander was, therefore, in no way extraordinary.

The Government's refusal to accept the proposal submitted by me gave me an impression that even though the hearings had yet to commence, the Government appeared sure that they would win the case ultimately. Considering that they had lost at two levels, and no new facts can be introduced at the level of the Supreme Court, their confidence left me with lot of apprehension.

The Government had been claiming that the Army Commander's is a selection post. I had to counter this. It is well known in the Army that when Lt Gen HB Kala was appointed Army Commander in 1996, his immediate junior, Lt Gen MR Sharma had put up a statutory complaint that his profile should be compared with that of HB Kala. However, the Government had rejected his complaint on the grounds that Army Commander's was not a selection post and therefore, there was no scope for comparison. This ran contrary to the Government assertion in my case. I decided to raise this issue. However, at the time MR Sharma was still in service and I considered it unethical to name him in my affidavit and thus cause discomfiture and embarrassment to a serving brother officer. Therefore in my affidavit, I put the matter in a circumspect manner. I took the line that since the Government is contending that it has been a selection post, there may have been occasions in the past when an officer standing second in the order of seniority would have complained against his non-consideration. I requested the Hon'ble court to call for such files and peruse to see how the complaint would have been disposed of. If that had been done, I had no doubt that Government's efforts to mislead the court would have come to light. However, the court refused my request on the grounds that I could seek perusal of records only dealing with my case and not others. My argument that the focal point was not I but the post of Army Commander and everything dealing with it had relevance did not carry favour with the Court and my plea was rejected.

There were a few more hearings after January 1999 but all these were of interim nature and had no significance. Each of these hearings was before a different Bench (comprising three justices). However, it so happened that each hearing came up before a Bench headed by the Hon'ble Chief Justice, while the other two members kept changing. This happened even though each of the hearings ended in an order that might have given an impression that the next hearing may be under a totally different Bench. Here are some examples:

Hearing on 18 December 1998

Coram : Hon'ble the Chief Justice
Hon'ble Mr Justice VN Khare
Hon'ble Mr Justice MB Shah

Order : *'Till the matters are listed before the Motion Bench in the month of January, 1999, the operation of the impugned judgments shall stay'.*

Hearing on 14 December 1999

Coram : Hon'ble the Chief Justice
Hon'ble Mr Justice M Jagannadha Rao
Hon'ble Mr Justice VN Khare

Order : *"...Let the matters be placed for hearing on 19.01.2000 before any available Bench..."*

In January 2000 my lawyer Mr PP Rao made an interesting observation. Quoting the Attorney who was representing the Government in my court case, Mr Rao told me that he (the Attorney General) had spent the Millennium New Year in Andamans and that Lt Gen HRS Kalkat had hosted the stay and had really 'laid in on'. It raised two questions in my mind. First was the question of ethics and probity in public life involved in the seniormost law officer of the Government of India enjoying hospitality of a litigant who in his SLP had made the Union of India a respondent? Second what was the source of funds for financing the visit? Did Kalkat bear the expenses from his pocket, or did he use official funds thus spending the taxpayers' money in trying to derive a personal benefit?

The main hearings in the Supreme Court commenced on 02 February 2000. On the first day, Kalkat's lawyer also made his submission, apart from the Attorney General. In his submission, the learned lawyer started reading from midway of an Army Headquarters letter that actually deals with officers up to the rank of Lt Col only and had no relevance in this context. After about 20 minutes, the Hon'ble Court asked him as to what was he trying to prove? After this the learned lawyer sat down and did not speak again throughout the proceedings.

A notable development on the first day was the court asking to be shown my ACR of 1971 along with that of Kalkat. To me this appeared a strange demand from the Court on the following grounds:

(a) We both had completed over 36 years service as officers and had earned more than forty ACRs during this period (including interim CRs etc). Perusing one of these reports that was more than 27 years old did not appear logical.

(b) While my report of 1971 was a war report, Kalkat's was not. This is clear from the 27 Mar 1998 Note of the Cabinet Secretary itself. For me the Note had said, 'In his report of 1971 when he participated in the operations…'. However, for Kalkat the Note had said, 'His report of 1971, the year in which operations took place…' Therefore, the Hon'ble Court was trying to compare two dissimilars.

(c) The High Court Judgment had already highlighted that I had some advisory remarks in my 1971 report and it was in the knowledge of the Hon'ble Supreme Court. Therefore, the Court was trying to compare two old reports where the outcome was already known.

(d) If the old reports had any relevance then what was the significance of picking up one particular report earned by us in the rank of Major and under dissimilar circumstances. The court could have as well compared our commissioning report where I had passed out 40 paces above Kalkat or any other report of 1962 war,

1965 war or of any year like 1976, 1986, 1993, etc., or, perhaps more relevant, our reports as Divisional Commanders in the rank of Maj Gen based on which Kalkat had been found 'unfit' by the selection board for promotion to Lt Gen whereas I had been found fit. They could have, and in fairness should have, also compared the reports of the years where Kalkat had received adverse entries in his reports.

(e) To my way of thinking picking up a particular old report from distant past and comparing it was like basing one's judgment on who was leading in the 9th lap in a 40-lap race and deciding the winner; or like deciding some one's college admission based on his class II results.

(f) The Hon'ble Court was also apprised that the advisory remarks as shown in the Cabinet Secretary's Note were not a faithful reproduction from my report and had been doctored to make these appear graver than actual.

The above objections were duly raised but were rejected by the Court. Not only were our pleas turned down, the Court even asked for a copy of the two reports to be handed over to them after these were read out in the open court. We then requested the Court to also have read out my citation for the award of a Vishist Seva Medal on 26 January 1980. The President based on my operational performance in leading my battalion in counter insurgency operations in Nagaland from February 1978 onwards had conferred this award on me. Since operations against insurgents are an ongoing war-like situation on a day-to-day basis and the citation – written by the same IO who writes the ACR - would have commented on the same very qualities that were commented upon in my 1971 report. However, this request too was turned down.

Another point raised by the Hon'ble Court on the first day was whether there was any precedent when a junior Lt Gen with a longer tenure as Corps Commander was overlooked for the appointment of Army Commander in favour of a senior who had commanded a Corps for a comparatively lesser tenure. This point has no relevance because total length of command of a Corps is not one of the criteria for the appointment of an Army Commander. Besides, there are numerous examples where seniors with a lesser tenure as Corps Commanders were appointed Army Commaders, such as Gen Shankar Roychowdhury, Lt Gens Jameel Mahmood, Arun Gautam, SK Sharma and a host of others. Even Gen VP Malik had commanded a Corps for a lesser duration than his immediate junior Lt Gen HS Bedi whose name was not even considered for an Army Commander, leave aside resorting to any comparison.

Apart from the above-mentioned issues, most of the first day was taken up by discussion on my eligibility. Interestingly, since the Government had held me to be eligible for the Army Commander's post throughout, the Government lawyer could not and did not participate in the discussion. Kalkat's lawyer had already gone quiet as mentioned earlier. The discussion was, therefore between my lawyer, Mr PP Rao and the Hon'ble Court. Seeing the trend of discussion I could not help asking myself whether the Hon'ble Court was arguing the case of Kalkat, the case of the Government, or was playing a neutral role which should have been the correct course. At one stage towards the end of the arguments the Hon'ble Court even remarked that while conceding that with the grant of the waiver I had become eligible, but 'my actual experience was still less than one year'. I asked myself if this was not strange logic. A waiver becomes relevant only when the actual experience is less than the stipulated and the waiver is there to cover the shortfall. If after the waiver one still talks of actual experience, then the whole provision of granting a waiver by the government is rendered an exercise in futility.

The arguments on my eligibility spilled over to the second day. Towards the middle of the second day, to my relief, a member of the Bench turned towards his other colleagues and emphatically said, "He is eligible". That terminated the discussion on this subject. It transpired later that my relief was misplaced, because in the judgment the Hon'ble Court again found me ineligible because of - according to them - a shortfall by 23 days in my one-year experience even after the waiver.

The Hon'ble Court then came up with another point (on day two of the arguments). Declaring that so far they had not examined the case ("We have not even picked up the paint brush and the canvas is absolutely clear", is how they put it) they remarked that they were of the view that if they brought down Kalkat from his conditional appointment of Eastern Army Commander, it would hurt the morale of Eastern Command and if they did not appoint me an Army Commander, it would hurt the morale of 1 Corps which at the time I was commanding. They were, therefore, of the view that both of us should be appointed Army Commanders. The Court clarified that for the next vacancy (occurring on 1.10.2000) I should be appointed an Army Commander even though I would have one month less than the required two years residual service which, the Court suggested, should be waived. The Court wanted the Attorney General to check this with the Government and also asked my lawyer Mr PP Rao whether it was acceptable to me. Even without checking with me Mr Rao stated, "my Lord you are offering me a consolation prize". The Hon'ble Chief Justice then asked Mr Rao to check with me. I told Mr Rao that I needed to think it over. The Court agreed to this and the Attorney General and Mr Rao were asked to come back with the response during the next date of hearing.

Before I discuss the merits or otherwise of the proposal, let me dwell on the subject of morale, which the Court had brought in.

A petitioner approaches the court to seek justice. Justice comes through application of law. To bring in the perceived adverse effect on morale as a factor for consideration in dispensing justice, in my view, amounts to including extraneous factors into the process. Following additional points are relevant in this context:

(a) Speaking in a larger context, ironically, nothing is misused more often than the morale of the Army to score debating points by different people/agencies. It has become fashionable to use Army morale as a prop to win arguments. It is also a convenient shield to hide behind when accused of wrongdoing. One recalls how, when 'Tehelka' and 'Coffin scam' surfaced it was argued by some that an investigation into these episodes would hurt the morale of the soldiers. These efforts presuppose that since the Army is the ultimate resource available to the country to sort out all its problems – which it always does – public should shun doing anything that may hurt its morale. The apprehension is so overwhelming that the word 'morale' itself has become untouchable. As a result no one 'risks' even cursorily examining what would and what would not hurt the morale of the Army. Actually, nothing could be more insulting to the soldier, who 'wears' that morale every day, than an opinion by those out of uniform, that such-and-such would affect his morale.

(b) With all deference to the apex court, if morale was the main or the starting point of debate then court room is not the right platform to do so because no one outside the olive green uniform can really understand what factors raise or lower a soldier's morale.

(c) It should be recalled that right in the beginning, the Delhi High Court Bench had ruled that Kalkat should not be appointed Army Commander till a decision on my writ petition was taken. This would have ensured a level playing field. However, the Supreme Court at that time overruled the High Court decision and allowed Kalkat's appointment to be made, *'subject to the outcome of the writ petition'*. Now when the High Court had given that outcome and the Supreme Court, by their own admission, had yet to consider the Government appeal against the High Court decision, for the apex court to hold, that removal of Kalkat from the conditional appointment would adversely affect the morale of Eastern Command appeared to be pre-judging the issue even without examining the merits. Having appointed him conditionally that very court was now holding that very fact in support of keeping him in that post. In my view it amounted to the Hon'ble Court itself creating a situation that presented itself as a fait accompli.

(d) Do courts always consider the factor of morale while arriving at legal decisions? Did Hon'ble Justice Sinha of the Allahabad High Court consider the effect on the morale of the whole country when in 1975 he unseated the sitting Prime Minister of India on charges of alleged electoral malpractice? Surely, an Army Commander's appointment and morale of the Army are insignificant compared to the Prime Minister of the largest democracy in the world and morale of the whole nation.

(e) The morale, if at all, can only be affected when laid down rules and historical precedents are ignored by the Government in making senior appointments, which had been done in this case, as found by the High

Court. Logically, by enforcing rule of law morale can only be raised. To conclude that replacement from post of an illegal appointee would lower the morale of the force involved is difficult to comprehend.

(f) As it transpired, my petition was dismissed on 28 Jul 2000. I continued commanding the Strike Corps for 17 more months after that. During this period the morale of the Corps continued to remain high and the court verdict had no effect whatsoever on the morale of the Corps. It is empirically proved, therefore, that the apprehension of the Hon'ble Supreme Court that if I were not appointed Army Commander, it would affect the morale of 1 Corps, was not correct. Similarly, there would have been no effect on the morale of the Eastern Command if Kalkat were removed from the post of Army Commander that had been found to be illegal by the High Court.

(g) How does one conclude that the morale of the force would be affected whether it is a Kalkat or a Kadyan who heads the Eastern Command? If such logic were indeed to prevail, then the Indian Navy should have fallen apart when their chief, Admiral Bhagwat, was dismissed.

The subject of morale merits one more comment. It cannot be denied that the one person who can speak most authoritatively about the morale of the Army is the Chief of the Army staff. When in the 31 October 1996 Selection Board, the Government had arbitrarily changed my grading from 'fit' to 'deferred', this is what the Army wrote to the Ministry of Defence:

1. *The SSB held on 31 Oct 96 considered the following Maj Gens for their approval to the rank of Lt Gens in General Cadre:*

(a) *Maj Gen RS Kadyan*
(b) *Maj Gen NS Gill*
(c) *Maj Gen BS Malik*
(d) *Maj Gen HC Ganguli*
(e) *Maj Gen SG Pitre*
(f) *Maj Gen NS Katoch*
(g) *Maj Gen KK Ganguli*
(h) *Maj Gen R Karthikeyan*

2. *On scrutiny and discussion by the Board, chaired by COAS with all Army Commanders as Members, Maj Gen RS Kadyan was unanimously approved for the rank of Lt Gen and the other Gen Offrs graded unfit... Certain observations were raised by Ministry of Defence vide their note dt 08 Nov 96 which were adequately replied to. Inter alia the MOD had observed that Maj Gen RS Kadyan should be treated as a deferred case as he has not completed the laid down period of AE as Divisional Commander and also that his special report has been initiated by the RO. We had replied vide our note quoted above to say that waiver of AE in view of the fact that Maj Gen RS Kadyan had been delayed in his appointment as MA in France in organisational interest because of delay in decision to down grade the appointment of MA in France. The officer had represented against his retention beyond his tenure of 3 years as he apprehended that delay would come in his way for further consideration in his career. However, he was asked to continue beyond authorised tenure strictly in organisational interest and, therefore, it would be patently wrong to let the officer suffer for no fault of his. Waiver of AE and initiation of report by the RO*

are well within the authority vested with the Chief of Army staff. Past precedent of five General Officers in whose case waiver has been given was also quoted. Therefore, consideration of Maj Gen RS Kadyan is very much as per the existing rules and, therefore, he should be approved as fit by the Government.

3. ....

4. ....

5. *It is, therefore, very strongly felt that any change in the recommendation of the Board in respect of Maj Gens RS Kadyan and ...* ***would have serious repercussions on the morale of the officers community in particular and the Indian Army as a whole because people will lose faith in our sense of justice and equity which has been a hall-mark of our Army."***

(Emphasis added by the author)

Here was the Army chief himself saying that change of grading in my respect would have serious repercussions on the morale of the officers as well as the Army as a whole. Who would know better than Army Chief what affects the morale of the Army? However, the government rejected the recommendation of the Army Chief without batting an eyelid. Nor did the Hon'ble Supreme Court take heed of this warning of the COAS while considering my writ petition praying. "*Issue a writ of certiorari or any other appropriate writ, order or direction calling for the records of the Selection Board held on 31-10.1996 and the decision taken thereon by Respondent no. 1 and after examining the same quashing the deferment of the case of the Petitioner as arbitrary, unconstitutional and violative of Article 14 of the Constitution of India and further directing that the Petitioner be deemed to be promoted to the rank of Lt. Gen. with effect from 31.10.1996.*" And now we had the Hon'ble apex court taking a decision to keep Kalkat in his post - that had been found to be illegal by the High Court - not on any legal grounds or basis but on the supposition that replacement of an Army Commander who had been holding the post on a conditional basis, would affect the morale of Eastern Command. Was that justice?

The only other point of interest was my lawyer Mr PP Rao revealing to me that during that period (after the Court had made the offer of appointing me Army Commander in the next vacancy) there had been a call for him from the office of the Defence Minister, who wanted to speak to Mr Rao. However, since Mr Rao had gone out of station, conversation between the two could not take place. The fact that Mr Rao mentioned this to me, along with the fact that the two of them did not normally have interaction, left me in no doubt that the intended conversation would possibly have been concerning my case. I have no idea what the Hon'ble Defence Minister wished to convey to my lawyer.

When the hearing resumed on 8 February 2000, the Government lawyer accepted the suggestion of the court regarding my appointment as Army Commander in the next vacancy. However, I did not accept it and chose to continue fighting the case instead. Many officers, including Gen S Padmanabhan, who became the Chief of Army staff after VP Malik, later suggested that I should have accepted the offer made by the Court. They are all well meaning but most of them are still not fully familiar with the details of the case. My decision was well reasoned and I have no regrets that I took that decision, even though I knew at that time that rejection of the Court offer would 'annoy' them. Let me share my reasoning with the reader.

In fact the Court offer was not materially different from what I had mentioned in the proposal submitted to the

Attorney General in January 1999. The only difference was that while I had suggested that both, Kalkat and I, should be appointed from the same date (01 March 1998), the Court had suggested that I get a future date. The Hon'ble court was undoubtedly being generous in giving me the next appointment of Army Commander, but it did not address the issue raised by me in my writ petition. **My grievance was against supersession, in that a junior had been appointed ahead of me.** By giving me the next appointment that issue was not being addressed. My fight was not for a particular post or chair per se. Nor was my fight against Kalkat or any other individual. **My fight was to seek justice for myself and ask for the appointment that should have been mine based on my eligibility, my merit, government's own rules and precedent. My fight was for honour.** In my perception the Court's offer amounted to accepting that there was nothing wrong with my record or my professional competence – despite all those falsehoods inserted in my career profile. However, for some reason a junior had been appointed ahead of me and it was a fait accompli on which they concluded they could not do anything. If my record made me fit for the post, then why was I not being given my rightful place in the hierarchy? I had nothing against Kalkat staying in the post as long as I was given the same date of appointment as Kalkat's and my seniority over him was maintained.

To sum up, I did not accept the Court offer because I did not find it giving me justice. **It failed to appreciate that for a soldier honour is the most dear and he fights for that.** Accepting the Court's offer would have surely put me in an Army Commander's chair but would have amounted to my accepting a compromise with my honour. The sentiments were aptly summed up by my lawyer who, while rejecting the Court offer, remarked, "For a soldier an honourable death is better than dishonourable living".

It is interesting to note that while the Hon'ble Court did not accept 23 days shortfall in my experience as a Corps Commander (where a provision for a waiver exists in the Government letter itself), at the same time it suggested - and the Government readily accepted – that one month shortfall in the required two years in my residual service for becoming an Army Commander - where there is no provision at all of a waiver - be waived.

It is also pertinent to note that government acceptance of the court offer proved that they had nothing against me as far as my professional competence and fitness for the post went. However, they were chary of removing Kalkat from his conditional appointment to the post. This further seemed to reinforce the perception gathered from Jaswant Singh's conversation with Ranjit Sethi in March 1998, about sensibilities of the party in power. Such can be the compulsions of coalition politics.

The case was discussed threadbare for four days. When the hearings terminated on 09 February 2000, as a closing remark, the Hon'ble Court asked my lawyer Mr PP Rao that while they asked the Government to reconsider their decision, could Kalkat stay in the post in the meantime? Mr Rao agreed while remarking, "That is OK my Lord, provided it is time bound". The closing remark of the Court left me in no doubt that the judgment would be in my favour. I waited.

I am not aware how long the courts normally take to announce their judgments. (In my own case the High Court had announced their judgment in less than three weeks after the arguments concluded.) An item appearing on page 3 of *The Tribune* dated 11 August 2003 seems relevant in this regard. The news item titled, 'Verdict withheld is justice denied', and datelined Chandigarh says, 'Even though the Supreme Court has ruled that the "pronouncement of judgement is a part of the justice dispensation system" and "should be done without delay", verdict is still being pronounced months after the conclusion of arguments in so many cases'.

It further says, "The Supreme Court has ruled, 'On noticing that after the conclusion of the arguments, the judgement is not pronounced within a period of two months, the Chief Justice (CJ) concerned shall draw the attention of the Bench concerned to the pending matter...Where a judgement is not pronounced within three months from the date of reserving it, any of the parties in the case is permitted to file an application in the High Court with prayer for early judgement...If the judgement for any reason is not pronounced within a period of six months, any of the parties shall be entitled to move an application before the CJ of the High Court with a prayer to withdraw the case and make it over to any other Bench for fresh arguments. It is open to the CJ to grant the prayer or to pass any other order as he deems fit in the circumstances'."

I understand the Supreme Court usually takes only 2/3 weeks to pronounce judgments. However, in my case it took rather long. I had another apprehension. If the judgment did not come out till 31 August 2000, I would become ineligible in terms of the two years residual service rule and would be debarred by default even if the judgment went in my favour. When five months had elapsed, on the advice of my lawyer I filed an application requesting for an early judgment.

The judgment finally came out on 28 July 2000, more than twenty-four weeks after the hearings concluded on 9 February. The Hon'ble Court had dismissed my writ petition.

Supreme Court Judgment

The operative part of the 32-page Supreme Court Judgment, delivered on 28 July 2000 is given ensuingly. I have also added my explanatory comments wherever, I felt, these were warranted.

The matter put before this Court in the light of the arguments advanced on behalf of the parties and the pleadings raised or the findings recorded by the High Court, we have to consider the same from five facets of the case:

(i) Whether the Army Commander holds a selection post or one which is based on seniority but the officer should be fit in every respect for such appointment and should have a minimum of two years before retirement from the date of appointment as Army Commander/VCOAS?

(ii) Whether the instructions given on October 16, 1992 are executive instructions not supportable in law which stipulate that an officer to be eligible to the post of Corps Commander should either be eligible to become an Army Commander or should have a minimum of four years residual service on the date he is promoted to the rank of Lt General and should have commanded a Corps for at least one year?

Comment : There is an unfortunate mix up here, between two letters. The eligibility for the appointment of a Corps Commander is given in the 16 October 1992 letter, which is a departmental letter, issued by the Army Headquarters. On the other hand the requirement of one-year command of a Corps is an eligibility condition for appointment as an Army Commander laid down vide Government statutory letter dated 18 November 1996. The two letters and their contents are distinct and different. Unfortunately, it appears, the Hon'ble Court had perhaps not fully understood the whole issue.

(iii) What is the effect of the ACRs recorded by the Chief of the Army Staff?

(iv) What is the effect of waiver granted to Lt. General R.S. Kadyan when he was a Brigadier serving in the Embassy of France?

Comment : No waiver was needed or ever sought or granted to me while I was a Brigadier. Before proceeding to Paris I had completed my required AE period in the rank of Brigadier and accordingly I was approved for promotion to the rank of Maj Gen in the selection board held in April 1992 in the normal course. This point was never brought up nor ever discussed in the courts and it is not understood how this got included as one of the facets. Also, after being listed here, this point finds no mention subsequently in the Judgment. To my bad luck, as a result of this error, it appears the Hon'ble Court may have perhaps formed an impression that I have been receiving waivers even in earlier ranks. This opens the possibility that the Hon'ble Court may have perhaps developed a prejudice against me.

(v) Whether the Cabinet Secretary is justified in taking into consideration the service profiles of Lt.General R.S. Kadyan and Lt. General H.R.S. Kalkat in making his recommendations?

Several decisions have been cited before us on either side by the learned counsel appearing in this case but we are not averting to the same since we are not in any way detracting from the principles stated therein nor are we enunciating any new principle. Moreover, we are deciding on the special features arising in this case.

On October 20, 1986 criteria of appointment of Army Commander was issued purported to be under the orders of the President of India and such criteria is as follows:

(a) The officer should be fit in every respect for appointment; and

(b) The officer should have a minimum of two years left before the retirement age from the date of appointment as Army Commander/VCOAS.

(c) *This will be applicable w.e.f. 1.1.1988.*

(d) *As a one time exception, the pay but not the status of an Army Commander will be given to those General Officers, presently holding the rank of Lt. Gen., who are otherwise found fit to hold the appointment but* ***are not selected because of the revision in the criteria.***

(e) *The officer should have commanded a Corps for at least one year so as to become eligible for appointment as Army Commander/VCOAS. No waiver in this stipulation will be allowed without prior concurrence of the Government. [added on November 18, 1996 pursuant to letter No. 19(24)/96/D(MS) issued by Government of India, Ministry of Defence.]*

(Emphasis supplied)

On the basis of this letter the argument advanced before us is that the appointment to the post of Army Commander is of selection and not a mere promotion on the basis of seniority. It is urged on behalf of the Union of India and Lt. General H.R.S. Kalkat that the post of Army Commander is a selection post and not a post merely based on seniority. While Shri P.P. Rao, learned senior Advocate for the contesting respondent, submitted that what is required in this letter is only that a concerned officer should be fit in every respect and should have fulfilled the other requirements. Though diametrically opposite views are stated, on a careful reading of this letter it becomes clear that "an officer should be fit in every respect for such appointment" will not merely mean that he must be physically fit or mentally fit but in every other respect. In addition in clause (d) above in the letter while making certain exceptions what was in the mind of the authority is made clear that an officer holding the rank of Lt.

General who is otherwise fit but not selected because of the revision of criteria will be a clear indication that it is a selection and not a mere promotion on the basis of seniority. Further, the expression "fit" has been brought to our notice as legally meaning "fit to be chosen" by elaborating the expression "eligible" in Stroud's Judicial Dictionary, 5th Edn. However, the expression "fit", which has different shades of meanings, also means "a person to be appointed shall be legally eligible" and "eligible" has been explained by us to mean "fit to be chosen". Again, the expression "select" means "chosen or picked up". Therefore we are of the view that to the post of Army Commander, selection has to take place. Of course, considering the nature of rigorous standards adopted in the matter of selection of officers from the stage of Lt. Colonel onwards upto the stage of Lt. General in the usual course it may be that the senior most officer is selected as the Army Commander. But that does not debar the Chief of the Army Staff or the Union of India in making the selection of any other person for good reasons who fulfils the necessary criteria. Therefore, we are of the opinion that it was improper on the part of the High Court to have concluded that the post of Army Commander is a non-selection post. Further, the conclusion reached by the High Court that appointment to the post of Army Commander has to be made on the basis of seniority alone cannot be accepted.

Comment: The observation of the Hon'ble Court, 'Though diametrically opposite views are stated, on a careful reading of this letter it becomes clear that "an officer should be fit in every respect for such appointment" will not merely mean that he must be physically fit or mentally fit but in every other respect seems to imply that I have been found wanting in my fitness in some other respect. It surprises me greatly. The COAS found me fit for appointment of Army Commander and for promotion to the next rank (that of a General). So did the Cabinet Secretary in his 27 March 1998 note to the PM and so did the ACC. None of the recommending or the appointing authority found or mentioned anything that could cast any aspersion on my fitness for the post of Army Commander. If the Hon'ble Court found otherwise, it was not unreasonable for me as the affected party to expect them to specify the respect/s in which they have found deficiency in my fitness. No such mention has been made in their judgment.

The 20 October 1986 letter of the Government had four clauses i.e. (a) to (d). The existence of the semi-colon as well as the word 'and' at the end of clause (a) and of full stop at the end of clause (b), clearly indicate that there are only these two requirements for eligibility to become an Army Commander. Clause (c), which lays down the date of applicability of the letter and clause (d) that lays down a one-time exception for those immediately affected, are merely administrative instructions and do not form part of the rules of eligibility. Nevertheless, I cannot have any legal disagreement with the Hon'ble Court if it picks out the word 'selected' from clause (d) and concludes that what was in the mind of the authority was that it is a selection post. But I will make a few comments.

First, if this indeed was in the mind of the authority, then how is it that they never exercised it throughout the history of the Indian Army except in my case? Even after I was thus discriminated, they have continued to follow the 'seniority-cum-fitness' rule and have been appointing as Army Commander the seniormost fit Lt Gen **without exception.** Not only this, as brought out earlier, prior to my case, when Lt Gen HB Kala was appointed Army Commander in 1996 on a single name basis, the next-in-seniority Lt Gen MR Sharma had filed a statutory complaint seeking consideration of his name along with that of Kala. The Government rejected his complaint on the grounds that the

Army Commander's was not a selection post and no comparison was called for. These grounds for rejecting Sharma's complaint still lie buried in the Ministry's files. In my case the Government took a totally opposite view and misled the Court by concealing the basis for their earlier decision. One may, therefore, conclude that irrespective of the use of the word 'selected' in their 20 October 1986 letter, the framers of that letter were quite clear in their mind that it was not a selection post.

Secondly, it needs to be pointed out that prior to the issue of 20 October 1986 letter, the eligibility criteria for the Army Commander was fitness and one year residual service. This letter only changed the second criterion from 'one year' residual service to 'two years' residual service. Therefore, when the Government said in clause (d) of their 20 October 1986 letter 'not selected because of the revision in the criteria' they were obviously using the word selection even for simple arithmetical calculation of the residual service. There was no hint of any comparison of merit. Technically, even when there is only one incumbent for the post, 'selection' is involved. The term 'selection' as used in the Government letter is a process and does not involve comparison between two or more contenders.

Thirdly, the Hon'ble Court's observation, '*Of course, considering the nature of rigorous standards adopted in the matter of selection of officers from the stage of Lt. Colonel onwards upto the stage of Lt. General in the usual course it may be that the senior most officer is selected as the Army Commander*', is difficult to understand. Only an officer of the rank of Lt Gen can be appointed to the post of an Army Commander. And all Lt Gens have to come up through the same path of rigorous standards of five selection boards before they reach this rank. There are no short cuts. Both Kalkat and I had come through the same rigorous standards. (The only difference was that while I had attained all my select-rank promotions from the rank of Lt Col onwards in the first chance, Kalkat had been rejected for promotion from Maj Gen to Lt Gen in the first chance and was so selected during a second chance through consideration of his statutory complaint. If anything, this tilts the balance in my favour when a comparison is resorted to.) Therefore, having concluded that the post of Army Commander is a selection post – which makes comparison between contenders mandatory – how can the Hon'ble Court in the same paragraph take a contradictory view and say that in the usual course it may be that the senior most officer is selected as the Army Commander? In so saying the Hon'ble Court appears to imply that you pick up the seniormost, consider him singly and 'select' him for the post. Also, this runs counter to their own inference, that it is not a post based merely on seniority. Additionally, if in their view, '*in the usual course it may be that the seniormost officer is selected as the Army Commander*', then why was I not 'selected' being the seniormost? The Hon'ble Court is in fact thus permitting seniority-cum-fitness to be followed selectively. I asked myself whether this would not permit the Government a licence to continue appointing the seniormost fit Lt Gen as Army Commander in future, having singled me out for discrimination? That is exactly what has happened. All the Army Commanders – **without exception** – appointed after my case have been so appointed based on the principle of seniority-cum-fitness. It was only I who was denied my fundamental right of equal opportunity.

It had been repeatedly stressed by the High Court and also by my lawyer in the Supreme Court that the seniormost officer considered fit for the post of Army Commander is to be so appointed. Therefore, the observation of the Hon'ble Supreme Court that 'the conclusion reached by the High Court that appointment to the post of Army Commander has to be made on the basis of seniority alone cannot be accepted' does not appear to be factually correct. To substantiate my contention and to enable the reader to conclude whether the observation made by the Supreme Court was factually correct or otherwise, let me quote verbatim all the relevant portions of the 64-page High Court judgment where this point has figured:

Page 40

Fitness in every respect coupled with seniority is the criteria of appointment to the post of Army Commander. Even the basis on which Lt. Generals IJ Khanna, Maya Dass and GL Bakshi were superseded, was on the ground that these three general officers were not recommended for their promotion in the ACRs and they did not meet the criterion laid down in the letter dated 20.10.1986.

Page 48

The controversy, which has arisen, can be shortened if we see the basic criterion for promotion to the rank of Army Commander. The requirement is that the senior most Lt. General, who is fit in all respects, be made Army Commander.

Page 50

From the plain dictionary meaning of word 'Fit', one has to see as to what is the requirement for promotion to the post of Army Commander. As per the criteria the officer should be senior most as well as fit in all respects.

Page 54

The whole case revolves around whether in terms of criteria mentioned for promotion as Army Commander, the criteria is seniority-cum-fitness or merit-cum-seniority. Supreme Court in State of Mysore vs. C Syed Mahmood & Ors. 1968(3) scr 363, while interpreting rule 4(3)(b) of the Mysore State Civil Services General Recruitments Rules, 1957, which required promotion to be made by selection on the basis of seniority-cum-fitness observed:

The rule required promotion to be made by selection on the basis of seniority subject to the fitness of the candidate to discharge the duties of the post from among persons eligible for promotion.

If the aforesaid rule is strict rule of promotion of seniority coupled with fitness then promotion is a matter of course.

Page 55

In the case before me, the criteria is not 'seniority-cum-merit' but 'seniority-cum-fitness', therefore, what is obligatory is that the promotion is automatic. Seniority-cum-fitness is not synonymous with seniority-cum-merit. Fitness is referable only to materials available in the service records. Any other material, which was taken into consideration, is extraneous where seniority-cum-fitness is the yard-stick in promotion.

Page 60

The whole rationale of the principle of seniority-cum-fitness is that seniority should determine the order in which an officer of a particular grade should be considered for promotion. Those considered unfit may be passed over. This means the seniority-cum-fitness principle and what it implies is that the senior person unless unfit should get the promotion automatically. Under the principle seniority ought to have been given preponderating weight.

The two-page judgment given by the High Court Bench also expressed similar views. Relevant extracts are given below:

> *It would have been a different matter if the senior most officer had been found not to be fit in every respect and in that eventuality, the authorities would have considered the next senior officer who may be eligible. However, that is not so. The writ petitioner was not held to be unfit in terms of the circular dated 20th October, 1986 ...*
>
> *We are also in agreement with the opinion of learned Single Judge that in past too, single person was considered and if not fit then alone the next in seniority was considered...*
>
> *In the present case, the criteria is not even seniority-cum-merit. It is seniority-cum-fitness which in other words means seniority subject to rejection of unfit...*

From the above the reader may decide whether the judgment of the High Court talked only of seniority, or of 'seniority coupled with fitness' while referring to the appointment of Army Commander.

The Supreme Court Judgment continues:

The next question, which we have to consider, is what is the nature of the executive instructions that have been given. Even if we accept the view given by the High Court that Army Headquarters communication in this regard merely amounted to an executive instruction and not supported by any orders made by the President of India, the learned Attorney General submitted that the other parameters that are clearly laid down in the letters of Government of India should be strictly followed, that is, all officers who are likely to be eligible for an Army Commander appointment in terms of two years residual service will have to be given command of a Corps and unless such officer has commanded a Corps for at least one year he cannot be considered for promotion. In the present case, respondent No. 1 became a Corps Commander on September 24, 1997 and the vacancy in the post of Army Commander arose on March 1, 1998 and thus he had not completed one year of experience as a Corps Commander and he had put in 5 months and 7 days experience and to this if we add the waiver granted by the Government in terms of 6 months, it will only be 11 months and 7 days experience. Even so, he falls outside the zone of consideration for being appointed as an Army Commander. However, much argument was addressed on the effect of the recommendation made by the Chief of the Army Staff and the order made by the Government of India in that regard. On January 6, 1998 the Chief of the Army Staff recorded a note in the following terms:

> *"In view of the above, I recommend that redress be granted to the Gen officer by way of granting 6 months AE waiver to him for consideration for promotion to the appointment of Army Cdr/VCOAS for a vacancy occurring on 01 Mar 98."*

The argument addressed is that the waiver granted by the Government is identical with the consideration of his case for appointment as Army Commander inasmuch as waiver has been granted for the purpose of considering his case to the post of Army Commander it is contended that his case should have been considered. We fail to appreciate this line of argument. The basis upon which the High Court proceeded is that having taken all the issues into consideration the respondents have taken a stand totally contrary to the recommendations of the Chief of the Army Staff as well as the Ministry of Defence. The absence of the concerned officer from India on an assignment in the Embassy of France, the waiver granted only for a period of six months and other various factors taken into account are also set out in the following terms:

'In view of the above detailed examination of the case, CAB is of the view that Lt. Gen R.S. Kadyan, VSM, be granted waiver of six months in tenure of GOC 1 Corps and considered for the appointment of GOC-in-C Eastern Command as the Gen Offr is not completing AE criteria due to :

(a) Delayed repatriation from France resulting in

(b) Delayed placement on criteria appointment for promotion to the rank of Maj Gen.

(c) Delayed consideration for promotion to the rank of Lt Gen and

(d) Revision of 'FIT' grading to 'Deferred' which resulted in

(e) Further delay in consideration, approval and placement as GOC Corps, and

(f) Application of new clause vide MOD letter of 18 Nov 96, the provisions of which only exclude him in 1962 batch vis-à-vis his batchmates.

All the above events were beyond the control of the complainant and were basically caused by the administrative constraints of the organisation. Hence, the Gen Offr deserves the benefit of grant of waiver in terms of natural justice and equal rights, clause of the law."

But whatever may be the circumstances or the period for which he fell short the waiver granted is only for a period of six months. If that is so, respondent No. 1 cannot be said to have completed the period of one year of experience as Corps Commander. Further, Lt. General R.S. Kadyan was considered by the Selection Board and found fit on April 10, 1997 but he could not be promoted as Lt. General and appointed as Corps Commander because of stay order passed by the Delhi High Court in the writ petition filed by Lt. General H.S. Bagga. The said order was vacated and thereafter Lt. General R.S. Kadyan was promoted on September 24, 1997 and he functioned as Officer In-charge 1 Corps with effect from August 23, 1997 without any effect on promotion, pay or any related benefits till he was promoted on September 24, 1997. Lt. General R.S. Kadyan was appointed as GOC 1 Corps after the stay was vacated on September 24, 1997. Hence that period including the period of waiver falls short of the requisite period of two years.

Comment: It needs to be recalled as to why the waiver had to be sought and granted to me. There was only one purpose, and that was to make me eligible for the post of Army Commander by waiving off whatever shortfall there was in the required one-year command of a Corps. The only vacancy of Army Commander for which I could have been eligible was the one that occurred on 01 March 1998. (For the next vacancy that was to have occurred on 01 October 1998, I would have become ineligible in terms of the two years residual service rule). As brought out above while recommending the waiver the Chief of the Army Staff had said in his note dated 06 January 1998, *"In view of the above, I recommend that redress be granted to the Gen officer by way of granting 6 months AE waiver to him for consideration for promotion to the appointment of Army Cdr/VCOAS for a vacancy occurring on 01 March 98."* And the waiver granted by the government clearly said, *"...In the light of the same and to meet the ends of justice, the Central Government in consonance with the prayer of the* *officer in para 23(b) and the recommendation of the COAS agrees to grant him waiver of 6 months..."* Therefore, it is obvious that the date 01 March 1998 was crucial in this regard. The period of 6 months was only subordinated to it. If with the six months waiver I was still to remain short by 23 days, as the Hon'ble Supreme Court have concluded, then it amounted to no waiver at all and the whole exercise of granting me waiver was wasteful and a mere eye-wash. In my statutory complaint dated 05 October 1997, I had simply asked for a waiver, which could bring me into the zone of eligibility for the Army Commander's post occurring on 01 March 1998. I had not specified any period for which this waiver was sought. The Army Chief had obviously, and rightly, counted the period from 23 August to 23 September 1998 (when I held the rank of Maj Gen) as my valid experience in the post of a Corps Commander, and therefore had found a waiver of six months adequate to cover the shortfall. After all, the experience relates to a person by virtue of the duties he is performing and not to the badges of rank he wears on his shoulders while performing that duty. And I had been performing all the duties of a Corps Commander as set out in Paragraph 12 of the Defence Services Regulations, Regulations for the Army, from 23 Aug 1997 onwards.

The Cabinet Secretary in his note dated 27 March 1998 put up to the Prime Minister had clearly stated: *On his submission of statutory complaint to the Government, requesting for waiver in this requirement, the Raksha Mantri, on the recommendation of the Chief of the Army staff, has granted a waiver of six months and thus he has also become eligible for appointment as Army Commander."*

In their affidavit filed before the High Court on 18 April 1998 the Government had repeatedly stated that with the grant of the waiver I too had become eligible. Even Lt Gen

Kalkat had accepted my eligibility throughout the High Court proceedings.

It needs to be pointed out that, as already mentioned, while deciding that the post of Army Commander was a selection post, the Hon'ble Supreme Court had picked out the word 'selected' from clause (d) of the 20 October 1986 letter and concluded, ' *In addition in clause (d) above in the letter while making certain exceptions what was in the mind of the authority is made clear that an officer holding the rank of Lt. General who is otherwise fit but not selected because of the revision of criteria will be a clear indication that it is a selection and not a mere promotion on the basis of seniority.'* (Emphasis supplied). This was so concluded despite the fact that not even once in the history of the Indian Army had the government implemented what according to the Hon'ble Court was in their mind. As opposed to this, while deciding on my eligibility, despite the fact that it was clearly not only in the mind of the government but also in their notings and pleadings that I was eligible, the same Hon'ble Court found me ineligible. In one judgment the Hon'ble Court has taken two diametrically opposite decisions. It was unfortunate for me that both the decisions have gone against me.

It is also relevant to recall that during the lengthy discussion on the subject of my eligibility vis-à-vis the period of waiver, one Hon'ble member of the Bench had clearly stated that I was eligible. Only when that was established, did the discussion progress to other points. If the court had not given that indication, we could have argued, on another prayer of my writ petition, namely:

(h) Issue a writ of certiorari or any other appropriate writ, order or direction calling for the records of the Selection Board held on 31.10.1996 and the decision taken thereon by Respondent No 1 and after examining the same quashing the deferment of the case of the Petitioner as being arbitrary, unconstitutional and violative of Article 14 of the Constitution of India and further directing that the Petitioner be deemed to be promoted to the rank of Lt Gen with effect from 31.10.1996.

Reader may recall that in the Selection Board held on 31 October 1996, the Board had unanimously graded me 'fit' whereas the Government arbitrarily – and without assigning or communicating to me any reason – had changed this grading to 'deferred'. With the grant of waiver and my becoming eligible for the Army Commander's post on 1 March 1998, discussion on this point was not very relevant. However, if my eligibility was to be questioned by the apex court, this becomes a relevant issue. It is ironic that this prayer of mine was dismissed by the Hon'ble Supreme Court without any discussion. Nor have any grounds for dismissal been given in the judgement.

The Supreme Court judgment continues:

On 5.10.97, RESPONDENT No. 1 made a statutory complaint that his case should be considered on the basis of merit-cum-seniority subject to being found fit for promotion and ultimately prayed the following:

(i) The decision to defer his case in connection with the selection board met on October 31, 1996 may be reviewed and if he is deemed to have been placed in command of a Corps retrospectively from the date of declaration of the results of that Selection Board.

(ii) In the alternative, he prayed that the stipulation of commanding a Corps for minimum one year to become eligible for appointment as an Army commander under the letter dated November 18, 1996

may be waived in his case as the delay in his promotion seems to have been caused entirely in the interest of service.

The Chief of Army Staff recommended waiver of this stipulation contained in the letter dated November 18, 1996 limiting to a period of six months. Therefore, the conclusion of the High Court that he became eligible to be considered to the higher post does not seem to be valid nor the High Court was justified in proceeding on that basis. The conclusion of the High Court to that extent is erroneous.

Comments: The impression conveyed in saying, "*The Chief of Army Staff recommended waiver of this stipulation contained in the letter dated November 18, 1996 limiting to a period of six months*", does not appear to be in keeping with the recommendations of the Army Chief. The Army Chief had recommended six months waiver calculating the period from 23 August to 23 September 1997 as part of my experience and thus considering a waiver of six months adequate to bring me in the zone of eligibility. He had in no way laid a 'limit' of six months. This becomes clear by reading the wording of the Army Chief's recommendation dated 06 January 1998 itself: ".... *On detailed examination I find that delay caused was due to circumstances well beyond the control of the Gen Offr and were primarily due to administrative constraints of the organization. I also find that new clause of tenure of one year as a Corps Cdr affects only the Gen Offr vis-à-vis his batchmates basically due to delayed placement...*

...In view of the above, I recommend that redress be granted to the Gen Offr by way of granting 6 months AE waiver to him for consideration for promotion to the appointment of Army Cdr/VCOAS for a vacancy occurring on 01 Mar 98."

If the Army Chief intended to keep me still ineligible by a 23 days shortfall in the required one-year tenure as Corps Commander, then where was the need for him to mention that the delay (in my repatriation from Paris) was caused due to administrative constraints of the organization. And where was the need for him to say that the new clause of tenure of one year as a Corps Commander affects only the Gen Offr vis-à-vis his batchmates basically due to delayed placement ? Both these statements are in my support and could not have been included if the recommendation of the Army Chief for a six months waiver was to still keep me ineligible. The apex court has picked out the six months from the Army Chief's recommendation and omitted the crucial date of vacancy 01 March 1998 mentioned in the same sentence of the recommendation. Such selective quotes can only mask clarity.

I have already given a full copy of my statutory complaint dated 5 October 1997, in an earlier chapter. The reader would note that the word 'merit' occurs only at two places in the entire complaint. The relevant extracts are reproduced again:

Para 1

"Based on my merit-cum-seniority, and subject to my being found fit in all respects, I am eligible to become an Army Commander on 01 Mar 1998."

Para 22 (c)

"This delay effectively ensured that I would not complete commanding a Corps for one year before a vacancy of Army Commander occurred (on 01 Mar 1998) for which my merit and seniority make me eligible."

Unfortunately, The Hon'ble Court has picked out only a part of a sentence from Para 1 of my statutory complaint. Their quote, '*...made a statutory complaint that his case should* *be considered on the basis of merit-cum-seniority subject to being found fit for promotion ...'* obviously leads one to conclude that I was seeking appointment as Army Commander on the basis of merit-cum-seniority. The complete sentences from my statutory complaint, as reproduced above, would clearly show that I was talking of my own merit-cum-seniority per se and not the principle of 'merit-cum-seniority' to be a basis as such. My complaint was not drafted by legal experts and I had used the term 'merit' as it is defined in *The Concise Oxford Dictionary* where it says "the quality of deserving well; excellence, worth; a thing that entitles one to reward or gratitude; good deeds as entitling to a future reward", etc. There is no mention of comparison of any kind. By an unfortunate omission of the crucial word 'my' occurring at both places in my complaint, an altogether different meaning appears to have been drawn than what was in my words and in my mind.

The Hon'ble Supreme Court has also found fault with the High Court for, *'the conclusion of the High Court that he became eligible to be considered to the higher post does not seem to be valid nor the High Court was justified in proceeding on that basis. The conclusion of the High Court to that extent is erroneous.'* The conclusion is drawn only when there is a consideration/debate/discussion or a disagreement between contending parties. As brought out above, in the High Court my eligibility was an accepted fact by all the respondents, including Lt Gen Kalkat and no one had complained against it. My eligibility was thus a non-issue in the High Court and therefore they did not have to reach any conclusion.

The Supreme Court Judgment further says:

The ACR for the period 1.10.1997 to 31.1.1998 is to the effect that he considered him fit in every way to hold his present rank and also to the next higher rank. On this basis, it is contended that the Chief of the Army Staff having recommended his case in the ACR as fit for promotion could not alter the same subsequently and give a finding that such a recommendation will have a limiting effect. The position in law is that appraisal report or an annual confidential report is not the sole factor to be considered by the selection authority but one of the matters to be taken note of by such authority. We may advert to two decisions of this Court in this regard, namely, AVM S.L. Chhabra v. Union of India, 1993 (Supp.) 4 SCC 441 and Union of India vs. Samar Singh, 1996 (10) SCC 555. Therefore, we are of the view that heavy reliance placed by the High Court on the ACRs to reach the conclusion otherwise is not justified. In deciding whether a post is a selection post or not, one of the criteria to be considered is if it involves a comparative assessment of officers necessarily the element of selection is involved and, therefore, the post with which we are concerned is indeed a selection post although not totally ignoring a senior.

Comment: The requirement is that the officer should be fit in every respect. In the Army, an ACR is the only document in which an officer's professional fitness is indicated. It is a crucial document and the only record based on which an officer's further advancement in the hierarchy is decided. My normal ACR for the year 1997-1998 would have been due on 01 July 1998. Because I was due for consideration for the post of Army Commander, the Army Headquarters called for a special ACR covering period up to 31 January 1998. This was so because, my performance as a Corps Commander was to be appraised and the only medium to reflect that is the ACR. If the Chief of Army Staff finds me fit while endorsing that ACR on the evening of Friday 27 February 1998, and then changes his mind on Monday 02 March 1998, it falls under what the Court calls '*alter the same subsequently...*'.

It leads one to the obvious conclusion that such altering of mind over the weekend would have been based on some unknown, mysterious, and obviously extraneous consideration.

It is relevant to mention that the only document the apex court ever asked for during the entire hearings was an old ACR of mine that was written over 27 years ago. One wonders if an *'appraisal report or an annual confidential report is not the sole factor'* then why and how the Hon'ble Court themselves attach such preponderant importance to it?

If the ACR is not the sole factor and is only *one of the matters to be taken note of by such authority* to decide one's professional fitness for promotion, then the question arises what are the other factors that do so? Such factors, that have obviously gone against me, have not been mentioned anywhere by the Army, the Government or even the Hon'ble Court. Did I not have a right to know what those other factors were? In today's environment when the 'right to know' has become the guiding principle, withholding from me what has adversely affected my interests, can hardly be considered justified. Ignorance can only lead to speculation and the apprehensions that came to my mind vis-a-vis the fairness of making senior Army appointments - and would surely come to the minds of others who read this - could not have been healthful.

The last sentence of the above portion of the judgment is not comprehensible. It seems to convey an impression that since there is an element of comparison for the Army Commander's post it is indeed a selection post. This would by implication mean that if there is no comparison, it couldn't be a selection post. That is what I had been arguing. Since the Government had all along been appointing Army Commanders based on their fitness and seniority and without comparison, it is not a selection post. The Hon'ble Supreme

Court first held that it is a selection post and then concluded that (since it is a selection post) comparison has to take place. Here, in this sentence the Hon'ble Court appears to be countering its own logic.

Again, *'although not totally ignoring a senior'* is self-contradictory. If it is a selection post, where comparison is mandatory, seniority has no place. In all the five selection boards from the rank of Lt Col to the rank of Lt Gen selections are based on comparative merit, and seniority does not figure anywhere when comparisons are being made. However, going by the Supreme Court verdict, if seniority cannot be totally ignored, then the question arises why was it ignored in my case? I was eligible, I was fit and I was senior. Then what were the grounds or the considerations based on which I was ignored by the Government. Even after reading the Supreme Court judgment, which is the ultimate Court of Appeal, the answer to this question keeps eluding me. I keep asking myself what could have been the purpose of the Hon'ble Court in writing this sentence? Whatever it may have been, the outcome has been that after discriminating against me and after eliminating me from the post, this provision has left the door open for the Government to keep appointing future Army Commanders based on seniority (which is what in fact has been done) and no one will have a right to complain against non-comparison because of this provision.

Let me revert to the judgement.

In raising an argument that respondent No. 1 being the seniormost officer in the cadre was being considered for the next higher post. The post in question being a selection post for purposes of promotion, the contention advanced is that all the eligible candidates in that cadre should have been considered and consideration of only two candidates, namely, the appellant in one of the cases and respondent No. 1 alone could not meet the necessary criteria. This contention does not also hold water because no one else has made a complaint and the case of respondent No. 1 has been duly considered. Thus the argument advanced by Shri P.P. Rao on this aspect does not stand to reason.

Comment: This is the second instance where in the same judgment the Hon'ble Court has taken a totally contradictory stand. On the question of my eligibility, the Hon'ble Supreme Court has criticised the High Court by commenting, '...*the conclusion of the High Court that he became eligible to be considered to the higher post does not seem to be valid nor the High Court was justified in proceeding on that basis*'. This criticism came even though in the High Court no one had complained against my eligibility and going by the observation of the Supreme Court one assumes that the apex court expected the lower court to take a suo motu cognisance of it. However, on the other hand when I complained that if the post of Army Commander was indeed a selection post and comparison was required, then why was this comparison limited only to the two seniormost officers leaving out the other seven eligible Lt Gens, the Hon'ble Court has replied, *because no one else has made a complaint* . After all law is a matter of interpretation and it is not uncommon that an earlier judgment by the apex court gets overturned by a subsequent judgment of the same court. However, the same bench taking a contradictory stance at two different places in the same judgment may be a rare occurrence, if ever. By an unfortunate coincidence in this case too the two contradictory decisions had been given and both went gone against me.

The Hon'ble Court held the post of Army Commander to be a selection post. Hence a comparison had to be carried out to select the best. When I brought to the notice of the court that how is it that out of a total of nine eligible Lt Gens for the post of Army Commander that fell vacant on 01 March 1998, only two were considered to select the 'best'. The court ignored this anomaly on the grounds that the other seven had not complained. To a non-legal person it seems strange. Should the law, or does the law intervene only when the affected person complains? Taking a hypothetical example, would the courts let off a policeman, who witnesses a murder but does not act to apprehend the murderer because the victim had not complained? A related incident appeared in the Delhi Edition of the *Times of India* dated 14 February 2003. It read:

> "The south district police on Wednesday night registered a hit-and-run case for the accident that took place in Yusuf Sarai. An eyewitness had informed the *Times of India* that a cyclist was knocked down by a Gypsy accompanying a Haryana VIP's official Ambassador car. Both vehicles sped away after the incident. However, the district police has not been able to trace the victim yet. Police teams have not been able to trace the victim yet. Police teams have been sent out to look for the vehicles. The eyewitness, Dr Phillip Dayal, had noted down the number of the Ambassador car and handed it over to the police..."

Going by this judgment of the Hon'ble Court it leaves me wondering why the police was wasting their time and effort in registering a case and in tracing the erring vehicle when the victim has not complained; in fact when the news appeared, the victim had not even been traced. Can one conclude that the police are acting contrary to the law?

On the subject of acting without complaint, I would like to quote another related news item 'Panel flays Ferozepore SSP on sale of girls', appearing in *The Tribune* on Friday, 5 September 2003, and datelined Chandigarh. It read, ' The

Punjab State Human Rights Commission (PSHRC) has come down heavily on the Senior Superintendent of Police, Ferozepore district, by claiming that "no complaint in this regard" has been received in any police station in the district... "The SSP, Ferozepore, is off the track," observed Mr Justice R.L. Anand, member of the PSHRC. "He has tried to side-line the main issue" ... "If no complaint has been received in any police station from any aggrieved person with regard to sale or purchase of a girl or woman, it does not mean that the police should not be discharging its duty of checking the menace at its own level..."

In the case under discussion I had in fact brought the irregularity (of not considering the other seven eligible Lt Generals) to the notice of the Hon'ble Court.

And of course there was a valid reason why none of the other seven Lt Gens had complained. The whole Army has known all along that the post of Army Commander is a non-selection post to be filled on the principle of 'seniority-cum-fitness'. Throughout the history of the Indian Army the post has been filled on this basis. Therefore, the seven Lt Gens, being junior, did not perceive it to be an infringement of their rights against which they could complain, just as I had not considered it an infringement when my seniors were appointed. In fact all of those seven – except those who became ineligible due to the two years residual service rule – became Army Commanders subsequently when their turn came based on seniority. As already brought out, in the past only Lt Gen MR Sharma had filed a statutory complaint in 1996 when being Number 2 in seniority he wanted his profile to be compared with that of the senior most, Lt Gen HB Kala. The government rejected the complaint on the grounds that the post was a non-selection post and did not call for comparison.

Another unfortunate error that has occurred in the judgment is that the Court have considered the appointment to the post of Army Commander a 'promotion' instead of an 'appointment'. (The post in question being a selection post for purposes of promotion...is what the judgment says.) As per the Defence Services Regulations in the Army, promotion is only from one rank to the next higher rank. An Army Commander holds the rank of Lt Gen and is appointed out of the existing Lt Gens who have been already selected to hold that rank. Being in the same rank there is therefore no question of a promotion being involved. Promotions are by selection and by erroneously considering the appointment to the post of Army Commander to be a promotion the Hon'ble Court appears to have concluded that this too is by selection.

The fact that appointment to the post of Army Commander is not a promotion can be borne out by another example. For Selection Boards No 1 (Brig to Maj Gen) and the Special Selection Board (Maj Gen to Lt Gen), all the Army Commanders, the VCOAS and the Army Chief are members. The proceedings duly recommended are sent to the ACC for final approval. For the appointment of the Army Commander there is no selection board, simply because it is not a promotion or a selection.

The judgment continues:

Now we come to the last aspect of the matter, namely, the manner in which the Cabinet Secretary examined the service profiles of the two officers in question. For purposes of convenience, we set out the relevant portion of the note:

(**Author's Note** : The Supreme Court judgment has given only some extracts of the note put up by the Cabinet Secretary to the Prime Minister on 27 March 1998 (Hereafter referred to as the Note). For fuller understanding I am reproducing the entire Note. The portions included by the Court are given in italics while the portion left out by the Court are given in a different (SIM SUN) typecast.)

"No. 6/7/98 – CS(A)
Cabinet Secretariat

Consequent upon superannuation of Lt. General Ravi Eipe, on 28.2.98, the post of GOC-in-C has fallen vacant and is required to be filled immediately. The appointment of GOC-in-C/VCOAS is filled by an officer of General Cadre (Command & Staff) and the following criteria have been laid down for this appointment.

(i) The officer should be fit in every respect for such appointment.

(ii) He should have a minimum of 2 years service left before the retirement age from the date of appointment as the Army Commander/VCOAS;

(iii) He should have successfully commanded a Corps for at least one year.

2. The officers considered to fill the post of GOC-in-C, Eastern Command are listed at Appendix 'A' of the Ministry of Defence ID note dated 23.5.98. (Author Note: This could be a possible misprint; the correct date may have been 23.3.98.) Lt.Gen RS Kadyan is the seniormost officer who meets the requirement of residual service of two years, but he has not commanded the Corps for at least one year. On his submission of a statutory complaint to the Government, requesting for waiver in this requirement, the Raksha Mantri, on the recommendation of the Chief of the Army Staff, has granted a waiver of six months and thus he has also become eligible for appointment for appointment as Army Commander.

3. The Chief of the Army staff, after considering the suitability of the two seniormost Lt. Gen who fulfil all the eligibility conditions, namely, Lt. Gen RS Kadyan and Lt.Gen HRS Kalkat, has recommended the appointment of Lt. Gen HRS Kalkat as GoC-in-C, Eastern Command, based on his overall profile and experience and also keeping in view the organisational interest.

4. The service profiles of the above General Officers are discussed below.

Lt. Gen. RS Kadyan: *He was commissioned in the Rajputana Rifles regiment of the Infantry in June, 1962 and has held various Command, Staff and Instructional appointments. He picked up the rank of Lt.Gen. on 24th September, 1997 and started functioning as regular Corps Commander. The General has a balanced exposure in Command, Staff and Instructional appointments. However, his staff experience in senior ranks from Brig. onwards is only limited to that of Military Attache. He has no experience of working in Northern Command and Army Headquarters. Since 1980 he has worked for about 4 years in field areas. It also appears from his records that he did not participate in 1962, 1965 operations. In his report of 1971, when he participated in the operations, there are some advisory remarks both by the IO and RO as below: -*

> *"...should be bold and aggressive in operations...Should lead his men personally to difficult objectives." (remarks by IO).*
>
> *"........his performance as a Rifle Coy Commander in the recent operations has been satisfactory though not upto the expected level." (Remarks by RO).*

The overall profile of the officer, especially in senior ranks has been clearly above average. All the reporting officers gave him above average ratings with sprinkling of outstanding ratings.

As regards CI operations, the officer has handled the same as IG North, Assam Rifles, but he has not had experience of commanding a regular Army Division. His experience as Corps Commander is also limited. He is a graduate of Staff College and has also done higher command courses. He is recipient of Chief's Commendation, VSM and AVSM. He is medical category SHAPE-1"

"Lt.Gen HRS Kalkat:- *He was commissioned in Maratha Light Infantry in June, 1962. He became Lt. Gen in Feb, 1996 and since then he is commanding 33 Corps in the Eastern Sector. The general officer has rich experience in Command and Staff appointments. He has worked both in Eastern and Northern Commands including high altitude areas. Since 1982 he has worked for about four years in remote field areas in the Eastern Sector, especially the border areas with China. He has also held important staff assignments in Military Operations, Infantry and Staff Duties Directorates in the Army Headquarters. His instructional experience is however limited to junior ranks only and he has practically no experience of CI operations.*

The officer did not participate in 1962 and 1965 operations. His report of 1971, the year in which operations took place is quite laudatory. The overall profile of the officer, especially in senior ranks has been clearly above average. All reporting officers have given him above average ratings with sprinklings of outstanding ratings. He is a graduate of Staff College and has also done Senior Command and NDC Courses. He is also a recipient of AVSM. He is medical category SHAPE-1.

5. The Chief of the Army Staff is of the view, which has been shared by the Ministry of Defence also, that between the two officers, Lt Gen HRS Kalkat appears to have an edge in-so-far-as experience in the main task of the Army is concerned. Though Lt. Gen Kadyan is senior but his 1971 report is clearly inferior to that of Lt. Gen HRS Kalkat and also contains some advisory remarks. Lt. Gen Kalkat's Commands of Brigade, Division and Corps have also been in difficult areas for longer periods and his staff experience is also rich. Ministry of Defence has also stated that as regards the awards, there is no direct nexus between the awards and the promotion.
6. Raksha Mantri has approved. CR dossiers of the two officers are placed below.
7. I have given careful thought to the matter. In the normal course supersession at this level should take placc only when it is unavoidable. However, since Lt.Gen RS Kadyan is not only short of adequate experience of commanding the Corps but his report of 1971 also does not speak very highly of him; this therefore tilts the balance in favour of Lt. Gen HRS Kalkat, though he is marginally junior interse. I am, therefore, inclined to support the proposal made by the Ministry of Defence for the appointment of Lt.Gen HRS Kalkat as the GOC-in-C, Eastern Command on promotion. The COAS has made this proposal, approved by the Defence Minister. In view of the urgency involved, I request the Prime Minister to approve the proposal. Approval of the Home Minister in ACC would be obtained ex-post facto.

27.3.98

(T.S.R.SUBRAMANIAN)

PRIME MINISTER

Comments: Before I come to revealing how my profile was falsified and how the two profiles were coloured to make Kalkat appear better, let me make a few general comments on the Note:

(a) There are only three criteria laid down for the appointment of Army Commander as set out in Para 1 of the above Note. The sub clause (d) to the government letter dated 20 October 1986, from where the Hon'ble Supreme Court picked out the word 'selected' to conclude that *"what was in the mind of the authority is made clear that an officer holding the rank of Lt. General who is otherwise fit but not selected because of the revision of criteria will be a clear indication that it is a selection and not a mere promotion on the basis of seniority."* is not part of the criteria as per the seniormost government bureaucrat himself. It would be incredulous to assume that the Cabinet Secretary was not aware of what was in the mind of the authorities.

(b) The Note leaves no doubt that with the grant of the waiver I too was eligible for the appointment and that there was no shortfall of any kind in any of the three eligibility conditions.

(c) Despite the grant of waiver, the Cabinet Secretary has stated for me '*is not only short of adequate experience of commanding the Corps....*' This effectively nullifies the grant of a waiver, which has been rendered meaningless. Mention of this could only betray a mala fide intent. It is relevant here to mention that after my case there has been only one more Lt Gen (Shantanu Chowdhury) who was appointed Army Commander in 2002 by granting a waiver to cover up his shortfall of one year for command of a Corps. Did the Cabinet

Secretary's note in his case also mention that he *'is not only short of adequate experience of commanding the Corps .'?* If not, (and obviously not as the officer was appointed Army Commander) it only proves my point that I have been singled out for discrimination.

(d) The ACC is a 'Committee', which implies a collective decision by a body. The Note says, *'In view of the urgency involved, I request the Prime Minister to approve the proposal. Approval of the Home Minister in ACC would be obtained ex post facto.'* How can a bureaucrat take the Home Minister for granted? How can he state in such categorical terms that the Home Minister, who is number 2 in the country's political hierarchy, would sign ex post facto? The bureaucrat can only say so when a decision on the subject has already been taken at the political level and the Note is being put up to complete a paper formality to support that pre-determined decision. This amply proves what Mr Jaswant Singh had told Ambassador Ranjit Sethi in their March 1998 meeting about the ruling party's sensitivity towards the fact that there had been no Sikh Army Chief since Independence.

Falsehoods

An Army officer's dossier is a confidential document; even the concerned officer is denied access to it. It is held in custody by the MS Branch in the Army Headquarters. Whenever the dossier is sent up to the Ministry, it always goes under the authority of the Army Chief. Since the officer concerned has no control on it, he reasonably assumes that the documents pertaining to him are faithfully and truthfully processed.

I was horrified to read the falsehoods and the slants included in the profiles put up to the Prime Minister. I cannot describe the actions of those involved by any term other than the proverbial 'stab in the back'. Let me narrate some of these.

Sectoral Experience : It needs to be clarified that postings of officers in the Army are controlled entirely by the MS Branch of Army Headquarters. Individual officers have no control on where and in what assignment they would serve. (There is of course a provision that one can request for a particular station on compassionate grounds. I say with great pride that throughout my service of over forty years, I never requested for a posting, nor did I ever seek cancellation/ change of any posting.) Therefore, the experience an officer gains or lacks cannot be held against him. Having made that general comment now let me deal with the specific issue.

The Note says for me, '*He has no experience of working in Northern Command and Army Headquarters.*' This is false. I have served for a total period of approximately five years in different Divisions of Northern Command. In fact I have served and have had experience in all the Divisions in that Command except one. As proof I produced before the Hon'ble Court Army Headquarters letter No 52334/IC-13153/Gen/Org 9(A) dated 10 May 1999. The learned Government counsel came up with an interpretation that in saying, '*He has no experience of working in Northern Command and Army Headquarters*' what the Note meant was that I have not served in 'Northern Command Headquarters' and not in 'Northern Command'. Even if, for the sake of argument, one was to accept this rather innovative interpretation, it leads to more questions:

- For Army Commander, Eastern Command, what is the significance of having had experience of having served in a small township called Udhampur, that is the Headquarters location of Northern Command? As far as I know none of the earlier Eastern Army Commanders had served in Udhampur before being appointed to that post.

- The fact that the Government counsel was adding another lie to mislead the court becomes clear from the fact that even Lt Gen Kalkat has never served in Udhampur. If the 'Headquarters' of Northern Command is what they meant in the Note, then what is the relevance of mentioning this for comparative purposes when neither of us has served there? Also, if not serving in the Headquarters of Northern Command is considered some sort of a deficiency or handicap for an Eastern Army Commander, then why has it not been mentioned in the career profile of Kalkat?

The experience of having served in a particular sector or Command has never been a relevant issue for the appointment of Army Commander, and was being applied only in my case. Just to quote one example. One Lt Gen who was appointed Army Commander in 1994, had no experience of serving in Eastern Command and Southern Command as well in Northern Command north of Jammu. When he was appointed Army Commander, a second name was not even considered leave aside comparison. And by all accounts he made an excellent Army Commander.

Staff Experience : The Note says for me, *'However, his staff experience in senior ranks from Brig. onwards is only limited to that of Military Attachee'.* This is false. I was also on the staff of the National Security Guard (NSG) from April 1987 to May 1988 in the rank of Brigadier. As proof I produced before the Hon'ble Court copy of an NSG certificate dated 10 May 1999. When I highlighted this in the Court the learned Government counsel said that in the NSG I had served under a civilian and that is why that staff experience was not taken into account. Unfortunately, even this statement was false because in the NSG I functioned directly under a serving Maj Gen (P.C. Mankotia) of the Indian Army posted as the Commandant of the NSG Training Centre.

It is interesting to recall how I was posted to the NSG. After I had attended the Higher Command Course, in April 1984, I was posted in the rank of Colonel, in an instructional assignment in the College of Combat, which is a premier training institution of the Army. My turn for next promotion to the rank of Brigadier was not due till 1987 and I was looking forward to continuity in that station till then. However, I had finished only an year or so when out of the blue I received my posting order to the NSG vide Army Headquarters signal dated 11 June 1985. It read:

"firstly (.) Col RS Kadyan VSM...selected for deputation for National Security Guard (.) secondly (.) instr offr report HQ NSG comma Block... New Delhi by jun 28 (28) (.) thirdly (.) offr on probation for 90 days (.) during probation offr borne on str parent unit (.) fourthly (.) offr will be posted to NSG wef the date of successful completion of probationary period (.) fifthly (.) move in National interest (.) no representation (.) ..."

If the Government genuinely thought that the experience gained in the NSG was of no avail and that it was some sort of a worthless or negative input in my career profile, then I would like to ask the same Government as to why was I made a sacrificial goat by being 'selected' for a posting there? Instead, they could have and should have given me exposure in some other staff appointment. As I look back now, the assignment that was given to me to serve national interest, and against which I was not even allowed the right to represent, was held against me for my subsequent career progression. Any government or organisation that acts in this manner can only be termed exploitative and cannot obviously inspire confidence amongst its members.

Advisory Remarks : The Note ascribes this remark in one of the (27 years old) ACRs of mine, *"....should be bold and aggressive in operation...." (Remarks by IO).*

I was shocked and aghast when I read this. The remark is not an exact reproduction from my ACR. The actual remark was 'should be bold and more aggressive in operations. This remark did not imply that my approach was not aggressive; it merely implied that I needed to be 'more' aggressive in my operational approach. That is why this remark had never come in my way of any of the five select promotions since it was written. The Army and the Government were fully aware of this. However, when the remark was put to the Prime Minister, it was doctored and the word 'more' was taken out to make the remark appear more serious than it was intended by the IO who endorsed it. It is also important to remember that a paper that has to be put up to the Prime Minister must be being checked at numerous levels at the Army Headquarters, the Ministry of Defence and the Cabinet Secretariat. It cannot, therefore, be a 'typing' or 'clerical' error. Such an error in a document of this nature can only be deliberate and can occur when everyone in the chain – or more likely the entire chain - colludes in supporting a pre-determined decision.

When it was pointed out to the Hon'ble Court that the advisory remark put up to the ACC and being shown to the Court through the Cabinet Secretary's Note, is not a true extract from my dossier, even the Government counsel was not able to say anything in defence. This may have been so because while I had listed the other falsehoods out in my written submissions, that gave the Government time to think up appropriate lies, this point was mentioned for the first time during the actual court hearings. It is noteworthy that even the Government functionaries, despite their rich experience in the field, find themselves at a loss when required to cook up lies extemporaneously.

The Note also reproduces the following remarks purported to be written by the RO in the same report, "....his performance as a Rifle Coy Commander in the recent operations has been satisfactory though not upto the expected level. (Remarks by RO)."

This againt left me totally aghast. In case the RO or the SRO endorses any advisory remarks in the ACR, it is mandatory for these to be shown to and be signed by the ratee. However, no such remarks by the RO were ever communicated to me. After learning of these remarks from the High Court judgment dated 11 December 1998, I spoke telephonically to the Military Secretary seeking a copy of the extract, which I was supposed to have seen and signed. On his advice I wrote to him a letter on 19 Decemebr 1998 requesting for a copy of the RO's remarks. After protracted correspondence my request was turned down. I was informed vide Army Headquarters letter dated 18 March 1999, that my 'request for relevant portion of ACR 1971 cannot be acceded to as the same is not permissible under existing instrs on the subject'. I again wrote through an official application to the Military Secretary stressing that I now intended to file a complaint against these reported remarks for which I needed a copy. This request too was turned down. And I was informed that I could file my complaint without having a copy. This was of course ridiculous. Significantly, the Army Headquarters did not specify what these existing instructions were that debarred an officer from obtaining a copy of his own report that he himself is supposed to have seen, read and signed. Their stance convinced me that they had something to hide. The obvious inference is that these remarks were fabricated and do not actually exist in my ACR; if they could manipulate and doctor the advisory remarks by the IO it was not beyond them to do so with the remarks of the RO. In any case they had done the damage by misleading the Hon'ble Court.

When I pointed out this (about the remarks by the RO) to the court, the learned Government counsel kept waiving a sheaf of some papers and saying that I had represented against these remarks. Despite my assertion that I had not made any representation against any remarks by any RO, he kept repeating the same thing. How could I represent against some supposed remarks that I had never seen? The Hon'ble Court could have of course called his bluff and perused those papers to ascertain who was telling the truth. But that was not done. I am, therefore, not clear in the final analysis what the Hon'ble Court assumed to be the truth.

I would also like to make the following comments about the advisory remarks:

(a) My report of 1971 was an overall 'above average' report where I was clearly recommended for promotion to the next rank. By highlighting only the advisory remarks to the ACC and concealing the laudatory portion of the ACR gives a distorted portion. *Inter alia* the following remarks from the same ACR should have also been included in the Note to give the career profile a balanced look; '...Qualities of courage, zeal, resourcefulness are amply developed...Deals operational matters with patience and cool mind...'

(b) As brought out earlier in Chapter 1, the policy of Army Headquarters itself, spelt out in their letter No 04479/MS: Policy dated 21.10.1998, says '...*Also human imperfections mean that any officer, however, capable, can be advised to improve upon any trait in the quest for excellence. An officer who is clear above average bordering on outstanding can be advised to improve some facet of his personality so that he attains truly outstanding capabilities/performance. In this context, to treat any advisory remark as 'adverse' would be travesty of justice and completely off the mark...*'

(c) The only advisory remark in my entire career was endorsed when I was holding the rank of a Maj. This remark seen in the overall context of an otherwise above average report, was not considered serious and did not even come in the way of my promotion from Major to Lt Colonel and for all subsequent promotions. After this remark I attained five promotions, all in first chance without the remark coming in my way. Highlighting this to the ACC is difficult to understand.

(d) The advisory remarks are nothing more than an advice. If the advice is taken and the ratee shows improvement, these remarks cease to have any relevance.

(e) After I was promoted to the rank of Lt Col, I was posted to Nagaland in command of a battalion of over 800 men. Conduct of war-like counter-insurgency operations every day during my over 30 months of command in that area (February 1978 – August 1980), called for all the leadership qualities, including the traits on which I was advised in the 1971 ACR. That I must have improved became clear when, for successfully leading the battalion in these operations I was awarded the Vishist Seva Medal by the President on 26 January 1980. During the hearings I had requested the Hon'ble Court to peruse the citation for this award so as to get a more balanced picture, but the request was turned down.

(f) Again as a Maj General, I commanded our forces in counter-insurgency operations in Nagaland during 1995-97. The success of these operations can be gauged from two factual developments. Firstly, that the currently continuing ceasefire came into being during the last weeks of my two-year tenure there. Secondly, for my operational achievements in Nagaland the

President again honoured me with the award of an Ati Vishist Seva Medal on 26 January 1998.

(g) During Operation Vijay, even after they had appointed Kalkat as the Eastern Army Commander and during the pendency of the court case, I was continuing to command a Strike Corps of the Army that was poised for participation in the war. This could not have happened if, as is made out in the Note, I was found lacking in some operational qualities.

(h) If at all it was considered essential to bring to the notice of the ACC even the advisory remark of the past, then how is it that the Government concealed from that august body the two adverse remarks received by Lt Gen Kalkat in his past ACRs – one when he was a Major and the other when he was a Colonel. (The Government through an affidavit filed in the Delhi High Court had acknowledged the existence of these remarks). This amounted to discrimination against me.

(i) There have been many cases in the past where officers with advisory remarks have risen to the level of the Army Commander or even higher. There has been a case in recent history where an officer with advisory remarks in a couple of his ACRs in his record, rose to become an Army Chief and did a splendid job in that chair. I am saying this not with any sense of disrespect to anyone but merely to highlight the point that the advisory remarks are nothing more than advisory, and cease to have any meaning when the officer takes that advice and shows improvement in subsequent period. Only I was made an exception.

(j) When the Government accepted the suggestion of the Hon'ble Court that I could be appointed an Army Commander on a subsequent vacancy occurring on 01

October 2000, it left no doubt that the advisory remarks were not the reason for denying me the appointment in my own turn. There was obviously some other calculus.

To put the subject of advisory remarks in the correct perspective, let me make a final comment. The advisory remark written in my ACR was by an officer of the rank of Lt Col whose own experience, professional maturity and field of vision were limited. In fact he was not considered fit enough for any further promotion and was retired in the same rank of Lt Col. As opposed to this I am going to quote an instance of a Maj Gen (name being withheld) who was given very damaging report by an officer of the rank/appointment of Lt Gen/Army Commander with all his experience, knowledge, wide vision and maturity.

It transpired that the Maj Gen was given a weak report as a Divisional Commander, by his Army Commander based on which he was found unfit for promotion to the rank of Lt Gen by the Selection Board as well as by the ACC. The Maj Gen submitted a statutory complaint against his ACR and, as part of normal processing, the same was sent to the concerned Army Commander for his comments. A summary of his comments is given ensuingly.

(a) "In the Sand Model, the first operationally oriented event conducted by Maj Gen...around six months after taking over as GOC Division, he had little or no concept of how primary operational task should be tackled, and managed to thoroughly confuse the participants by indulging in semantics. The Army Commander had to spend 30-40 minutes in clarifying salient aspects of a...offensive on a...type obstacle system.

(b) In a war game some months later, Maj Gen...was somewhat confused and amongst others recommended launching his Division, to restore the situation, betwixt the enemy's two attacking Divisions to achieve 'surprise' by an unorthodox approach. In the event, his Division would have been wiped out by fire from both flanks since the gap between them was narrow and well covered.

(c) The Army Commander was present for another Sand Model Discussion in the Division, conducted as a prelude to an exercise with troops. It was evident that although the GOC (Maj Gen...) had grasped the general tactical considerations for the operation (since his first Sand Model Discussion) but his conceptualisation of operations, foresight in planning, and judgement in evaluating the situation and utilisation of resources were somewhat mixed up. The GOC tended to be carried away by irrelevant and confused logic while missing out on the essentials."

The Army Chief recommended rejection of the officer's statutory complaint. However, despite his recommendations to the contrary and despite such clear and strong adverse comments on the officer's professional competence, the Ministry gave him redress. When the officer's case came up for promotion to the rank of Lt Gen a second time, the Selection Board again graded him 'unfit'. However, the Ministry changed the grading to 'fit'. The Army Headquarters even pointed out to the Ministry... *'Despite clear adverse comments on officer's professional competence, he was given redress which unfortunately appeared arbitrary and discriminatory because many other General Officers who have career profiles as good as that of Maj Gen... have not been given redressal. Also the SSB while going through the entire record of Maj Gen... had noticed that he had weak reports as...*(Referring to his appointment in the rank of Brigadier-Author.) *Since reports as Brigadier are also considered by the Board, he was unanimously declared unfit... It is, therefore, very strongly felt that any change in the recommendation of the Board in respect of... would have serious repercussions on the morale of officers community in particular and the Indian army as a whole because people will lose faith in our sense of justice and equity which has been a hall-mark of our Army. We feel that promotion of one General Officer who apparently does not deserve it, is too high a price to pay in terms of its adverse effect on leadership of Indian army'.*

Despite such critical comments on the officer's professional competence by an Army Commander and despite such strong opposition from the Army, the said Maj Gen was promoted to the rank of Lt Gen by the Government.

The above would give a fair idea what importance is attached by the Ministry to adverse remarks given to a Maj Gen by such high ranking an officer as an Army Commander. Reader should be able to assess whether making an issue of my advisory remark that was over 27 years old, was genuine or whether it was a mere ploy to support a pre-determined outcome.

Importance/relevance of Awards: In Para 5 the Note says, '*Ministry of Defence has also stated that as regards the awards, there is no direct nexus between the awards and the promotion.*' The contention of the Ministry of Defence is factually incorrect. The awards have the same weight/nexus with promotions as battle reports have. This is evident from Para 12 of Army Headquarters policy letter dated 08 May 1980. Extract of Para 12 is reproduced below:

12. *Internal Assessment of all cases being considered and awarded in the Selection Board is carried out within the MS Branch under the directions of the secretary of the requisite selection board. The following aspects are seen:*
    (a) *Eligibility of the officer to be considered and awarded a definite grading. The following aspects are seen:*

i to v. *xxxxxx*

vi. *Battle report.*

vii. *Details of citations of award*

viii to xiii. *xxxxxx*

When the Note was written in March 1998, I had three awards to my credit, namely: Ati Vishist Seva Medal (for operational achievements in Nagaland in the rank of Maj Gen), Vishist Seva Medal (for operational achievements in Nagaland in the rank of Lt Col) and the COAS Commendation (for operational achievements in Operation 'Black Thunder' in the rank of Colonel). As compared to this, Kalkat had only one award of Ati Vishist Seva Medal (for the services rendered while serving in a non-operational post in the Army Headquarters in Delhi). In the above-cited policy letter both the battle reports and the awards are listed together. The only way the Defence Ministry could deny me the advantage of my three operational rewards was by falsely stating that these have no direct nexus with promotions. In fact the nexus is as direct as the nexus of ACRs with promotions. Despite this, while giving preponderant importance to my ACR of 1971, the Note negates my awards by averting to a factually incorrect observation of the Ministry of Defence.

Command of a Division: The Note says, *'...but he has not had experience of commanding a regular Army Division'.* This is contrary to the spirit of the Army's own policy and is misleading. In accordance with Army Headquarters policy letter dated 27 June 1996, for purposes of criteria appointment the appointment of Inspector General Assam Rifles, and that of Force Commander in the Rashtriya Rifles are equated with the Command of a regular Army Division. After my case, Lt Gens GS Sihota and Shantonu Chowdhury have both become Army Commanders without having commanded a regular Army

Division; they were both Force Commanders in the Rashtriya Rifles. One wonders whether a similar remark was also endorsed when their career profiles were put up to the ACC, or was I the only one singled out for this discriminatory treatment? I would also remind the reader that, as revealed by the Military Secretary during my interview with him on 25 August 1995 (details already given in an earlier chapter), I was specially hand-picked by the then Army Chief, to handle the difficult insurgency situation in Nagaland as overall operational commander in that State in the appointment of Inspector General Assam Rifles. I never myself sought the command of this so-called 'non regular' Army Division. How can one commend a system that selects an officer to handle a difficult situation, awards him for doing it successfully, and then holds the same assignment against him for his future career advancement?

It is interesting to note that without having commanded a regular Army Division the Government had no difficulty or hesitation in promoting me from Maj Gen to Lt Gen and giving me command of a Strike Corps. However, this was suddenly made out to be a handicap for an appointment in the same rank of Lt Gen. There obviously has to be something more than meets the eye.

Command of a Corps: To become eligible for the post of Army Commander, one has to successfully command a Corps. Till 1996 there was no minimum time limit for tenure as Corps Commander. However, on 18 November 1996, the Ministry of Defence prescribed a fresh condition of minimum one year of command of a Corps to become eligible for the appointment of Army Commander. As already brought out, this new policy was issued at a time when my selection board for promotion to Lt Gen had already been convened (on 31 October 1996) and the results were under finalisation. Besides, at the time I was the only officer in the entire Army to be adversely affected by it. In any case on my statutory complaint, the Government had granted me a waiver from this stipulation. With this waiver, I too became eligible. This has been so accepted in the Note by saying, '*On his submission of a statutory complaint to the Government, requesting for waiver in this requirement, the Raksha Mantri, on the recommendation of the Chief of the Army Staff, has granted a waiver of six months and thus he has also become eligible for appointment for appointment as Army Commander.*'

With the grant of the waiver and my having become eligible, the chapter of length of command of a Corps should have been finally closed. But that was not the case. In Para 7 the Note goes on to say, '*However, since Lt.Gen RS Kadyan is not only short of adequate experience of commanding the Corps....*' Once the shortfall has been condoned and I have become eligible, where is the need to keep harping on the same issue? It seems that the Government was not reconciled to the grant of waiver. They could not have denied it since such action would have been legally untenable. But having granted that waiver, they then rendered it meaningless by denying me the level playing field that the waiver sought to create.

When this point was brought to the notice of the Hon'ble Court, they wanted to know whether in the past there was a case where a junior officer who had commanded a Corps for a longer period was denied the appointment of an Army Commander and a senior who had had a shorter tenure as a Corps Commander was appointed instead. Since the total length of tenure has never been a criterion for higher promotions or posts, this point appeared out of context. However, since the Hon'ble Court had desired to know, many such names were submitted. These included, among others, names of Gen S Roychowdhury, and Lt Gens Jameel Mahmood, Arun Gautam and SK Sharma who were appointed

Army Commanders even though they had commanded a Corps for a lesser period than their juniors. Ironically, another name submitted was that of Gen VP Malik whose command of a Corps was for a lesser duration than his immediate junior Lt Gen HS Bedi and latter's name was not even considered when Malik was appointed Army Commander.

The whole thing comes back full circle. My tenure as Corps Commander was less because I was behind my peers in promotion to Maj Gen and thereafter to Lt Gen; I was behind because I was made to stay longer than required in France against my wishes; when the Army tried to remove that anomaly by holding my selection board, the Government arbitrarily changed my grading of 'fit' to 'deferred' without assigning any reason; and then they put another hurdle in my way by laying down a minimum tenure as Corps Commander; when that shortfall was waived, the Cabinet Secretary started talking in terms of 'actual' experience. It is difficult to avoid a conclusion that the system was hell-bent in promoting Kalkat's interests and getting an endorsement of the ACC on a pre-determined decision. When the umpire openly sides with one of the teams, how can one ever expect fair play?

Before passing on to the next falsehood, two more relevant points need to be made on the subject of length of tenure as Corps Commander. Firstly, prior to the issue of 18 November 1996 letter, several Lt Gens who had commanded a Corps for less than one year became Army Commanders. (In one case an officer actually became Vice Chief of Army Staff after commanding a Corps for just 94 days.) One of them even rose to become Army Chief. They proved to be as much competent as Army Commanders as those who had commanded a Corps for longer than one year. I am mentioning this to highlight that the 23 days shortfall in that one-year stipulation that the apex court ultimately found in my case, did not mean that it would have had any impact on my competence as an Army Commander. Instead, it was nothing more than a mere paper infringement of the newly introduced rule. It is strange logic that my experience of 11 months and 7 days command of a Corps was considered less enriching than someone else's 94 days' experience, just because my experience occurred after 18 November 1996.

During the hearings, the Court verbally admitted that I was eligible in terms of one-year command of a Corps. If they had not, I would have continued with the arguments on the subject and given other relevant facts till the Hon'ble Court were finally convinced. In the event of my failing to convince the Court, I would have argued on that prayer of my writ petition where I had questioned the Government decision to change my grading from 'fit' to 'deferred' in the Oct 31 October 1996 selection board. Unfortunately, with the Court verbally admitting and observing that I was eligible, I got scuttled on both counts.

Length/Difficulty of Command: The Note says, *'Lt. Gen Kalkat's Commands of Brigade, Division and Corps have also been in difficult areas for longer periods...'* It needs to be reiterated that which officer holds what assignment, in which area and for how long, is entirely decided by the system, and individuals have no control over it. Then how can such an irrelevant issue be included in a comparative assessment? Besides, even factually this statement was false. At least in command of a Division, my tenure was longer than that of Kalkat. Additionally, I commanded my Brigade on the Indo-Tibet border where for two years I lived at approximately 13000 feet above sea level, in a remote area. My command of a Division was in Nagaland where apart from a remote location, there was ever-present risk/danger of insurgent action on daily basis. It is a matter of perception whether these areas are more or less difficult than Tenga where Kalkat commanded his Brigade and Division and where permanent accommodation and related facilities exist and where there is no tension on the border.

The 1971 Report : The comparison of 1971 reports of Kalkat and mine was indeed a masterful stroke of deceit. Comparison is always between similars. Mine was a battle report. The Note in Para 4 admits this and says for me, *In his report of 1971, when he participated in the operations...'* However, for Kalkat, the Note uses linguistic jugglery to make it sound like a battle report. For Kalkat the Note says, *His report of 1971, the year in which operations took place is quite laudatory'.* It requires a few readings to catch that his report of 1971, is only of the year in which operations took place and does not indicate that he actually participated in these operations. This is akin to praising someone's patriotism only because he was born in 1947, the year in which Independence took place! That Kalkat's unit, 2 MARATHA LI, did not participate in the operations is a historical fact. That unit suffered not a single casualty due to enemy action, (my unit, 19 RAJ RIF suffered 79); did not get a single award (my unit won five gallantry awards); on the day of the cease-fire on 16 December 1971, Kalkat's unit was in Jandiala Guru in Punjab, having moved there from Bagdogra in the East on 11 December 1971. We had marched into *Dacca* on 16 December 1971.

Even the Note, despite its clever use of language, does not say that Kalkat participated in the operations. His report of 1971, therefore, was like any other report of any other year. Then what was the relevance of comparing this report with my battle report of that time? It was obviously to confuse the records and make it appear that Kalkat's battle record was better than mine when the fact was and is that Kalkat has never participated in any war in his entire service. Also, when a large part of our Army has been involved in countering-insurgency for the last five decades in various parts of the country, Kalkat has never been involved in such operations, as is clear from the Note, *'he has practically no experience of CI operations'*. As opposed to this, I have had six years of experience in counter-insurgency operations in Nagaland and Mizoram. The Eastern Command is responsible for handling the insurgency in the entire North-Eastern region of the country. If experience was any criterion, how could Kalkat be better placed than me is difficult to comprehend. In sum, in his entire service, Kalkat with no experience of war or counterinsurgency, has never heard a shot fired in anger, an acid test of any soldiering. Still, the Note through falsehoods and clever twist of language, makes him out to be better in comparison. Based on such Government decisions, if some ambitious Army officers start seeking 'perfumed prince' postings that carry no physical dangers and no professional risks, it would be difficult to fault their line of thinking.

Service in the Eastern Sector : For Kalkat the Note says, *'Since 1982 he has worked for about four years in remote field areas in the Eastern Sector, especially the border areas with China.'* I commanded a Company in the Eastern Sector, a Battalion in the Eastern Sector, a Brigade in the Eastern Sector and a Divison in the Eastern Sector. I have a total of over eight years service in the Eastern Sector. The two years of command of a Brigade was in Eastern Sikkim where we were in an eyeball-to-eyeball contact with the Chinese. Despite this, the terms 'Eastern Sector' and 'border areas with China' are conspicuously missing from my profile. The intention in the Note obviously was to make it appear that Kalkat was better qualified to head the Eastern Command, which has responsibility of a portion of the Sino-Indian border.

Service in High Altitude Areas : For Kalkat the Note says, *'He has worked both in Eastern and Northern Commands* *including high altitude areas.'* I have worked in high altitude areas thrice - in the Northern Command (Ladakh), in the Central Command on the Indo-Tibet border (Garhwal area), as well in the Eastern Command (Sikkim). However, the term 'high altitudes' is conspicuously absent from my career profile. I even produced before the Hon'ble Court copy of Army Headquarters letter No 52334/ IC-13153/Gen/MP6 (A) dated 10 March 2000, as proof of my high altitude service.

Staff Experience : For Kalkat the Note says, *'He has also held important staff assignments in Military Operations, Infantry and Staff Duties Directorates in the Army Headquarters.* This included Kalkat's assignment in the rank of Lt Col. However, in the same rank of Lt Col I held an operational appointment and was General Staff Officer Grade 1 (GSO 1) of an Infantry Division in the Western sector, which fact has been suppressed from the ACC in the Note.

Final Comment on the Note : I do not know at what level this Note by the Cabinet Secretary was prepared, and who injected these falsehoods into my career profile; whether it was in the Cabinet Secretary's office, the Ministry of Defence or the Army Headquarters. The entire record of an officer is kept in the custody of the Army Headquarters under the orders of the Chief of the Army Staff. The Army Chief enjoys blind faith of all officers and this is the hallmark of Army's culture and ethos. In reciprocation it should be incumbent on the Army Chief to ensure that records of subordinate officers are put up to the decision makers in the Government in an accurate and unbiased manner. **When the keeper of that faith himself orders or permits or overlooks manipulation of these records it comes as a betrayal of that faith from which the Army as an organisation draws its strength.** It pains me greatly to say this but I am convinced this is required to be said.

The Response of Hon'ble Supreme Court

All the above falsehoods were brought to the notice of the Hon'ble Supreme Court. It was argued that the comparison has been carried out on an inaccurate and biased presentation of facts to the ACC. The response of the Hon'ble Court is shown in the concluding part of the judgment that is reproduced as follows:

The contention put forth before us is that there are factual inaccuracies in the statement recorded by the Cabinet Secretary in his note and, therefore, must be deemed to be vitiated so as to reach a conclusion that the decision of the Government in this regard is not based on proper material. The learned Attorney General, therefore, took great pains to bring the entire records relating to the relevant period which was considered by the Cabinet Secretary and sought to point out there were notings available on those files which justify these remarks. Prima facie, we cannot say, having gone through those records, that these notings are baseless. Critical analysis or appraisal of the file by the Court may neither be conducive to the interests of the officers concerned or for the morale of the entire force. May be one may emphasise one aspect rather than the other but in the appraisal of the total profile, the entire service profile has been taken care of by the authorities concerned and we cannot substitute our view to that of the authorities. It is a well-known principle of administrative law that when relevant considerations have been taken note of and irrelevant aspects have been eschewed from consideration and that no relevant aspect has been ignored and the administrative decisions has nexus to the facts on record, the same cannot be attacked on merits. Judicial review is admissible only to the extent of finding whether process in reaching decision has been observed correctly and not the decision as such. In that view of the matter, we think there is no justification for the High Court to have interfered with the order made by the Government.

Before parting with the case we need to observe that considering the nature of the sensitivity of the posts involved and that each of the officer feeling that he did not get the best of the deal at the hands of the Government or that the members of the force being aware who is the best is not heading them will certainly weaken the esteem and morale of the force. Therefore, the standards to be adopted and applied should be of the highest order so as to avoid such an impression in the force.

In the result, we allow the appeals filed by the Union of India and Lt. Gen. H.R.S. Kalkat and set aside the orders made by the High Court and dismiss the writ petition filed by respondent No. 1.

(S. Rajendra Babu)
(Doraiswamy Raju)
New Delhi, July 28, 2000.

Comments: On the last day of the hearings the learned Government counsel did show one document to the Hon'ble Court. When this was being done my lawyer, Mr PP Rao, requested that the document be also shown to him. Mr Rao stressed the point that it was his legal right to see it. He even gave an assurance that he would not share it with me as his client. However, the Hon'ble Court did not permit him to see the document.

Since it was not shown, I have no idea what notings were shown to the court. I fail to understand what noting or notings could there be that justified inclusion of falsehoods in my profile? In any case by withholding from me something that has obviously gone against me, I was denied my right to defend myself. I am not a legal person but it appears that when a document is shown to the court and which goes against the respondent and the latter is denied access to it, it constitutes a violation of the principle of natural justice.

I am clearly intrigued by what could have been the contents written on that piece of paper. Was there a report against me by th CBI? Was there any allegation of my having been involved in anti-national activities? Was I trying to use political contacts, like Air Marshal Sekhon did? Was there anything else derogatory against me? Whatever it was, it was not in existence till I went to court as it was not mentioned in the Cabinet Secretary's Note to the Prime Minister dated 27 March 1998. Nor was it produced in the High Court till they gave the judgment on 11 December 1998. Even in the Supreme Court it was produced at the last minute after I had refused to accept the compromise proposal of being appointed an Army Commander in the next vacancy. Further, it could not have been in my dossier even after the Supreme Court judgment, otherwise they would not have appointed me a Deputy Chief of Army Staff in December 2001. Interestingly, the Government was willing to appoint me an Army Commander on 1 October 2000 despite whatever were the contents of this mysterious piece of document. I find it hard to believe that it was anything more than a very damaging document fabricated only for this purpose (of influencing the court) and it seems to have disappeared when that purpose had been served. It is most unfortunate that the apex court read it and even referred to it in their judgment, and were thus obviously influenced by it, but did not make it part of the court records and even refused to show it to my lawyer.

My regret is not that the political will of the time stooped to this level; with what I had experienced, I expected nothing better or different from them. My regret is that the apex court took cognisance of it.

I would also like to comment on the observation made by the Hon'ble Court in the judgment to the effect, '*It is a well-known principle of administrative law that when relevant considerations have been taken note of and irrelevant aspects have been eschewed from consideration and that no relevant aspect has been ignored and the administrative decisions has nexus to the facts on record, the same cannot be attacked on merits'.* I have no dispute with the principle of the administrative law. But in the absence of any criteria or guidelines for carrying out the 'selection' for the post of Army Commander (except the government letters dated 20 October 1986 and 18 November 1996), how does one conclude what is relevant and what is not relevant? Is scrutiny of a Confidential Report that was 27 years old relevant? Is staff experience relevant? Is service in difficult areas relevant? Is comparing two dissimilar reports relevant? Are operational awards relevant? Is service in high altitudes relevant? Is service in Northern Command Headquarters relevant for becoming an Army Commander of another Command, and if so how did it not come in the way of several others including VP Malik himself when he became Army Commander of Southern Command without having served in the Northern Command Headquarters? Is total length of tenure as Corps Commander relevant, when it did not come in the way of Shankar Roychowdhury, Jameel Mahmood, AK Gautam, SK Sharma, VP Malik and many others?

For all the selection boards for promotion up to the rank of Lt Gen, criteria that are to be considered are laid down. For the appointment of Army Commander, neither the Government nor the Army have (even now) laid down any criteria or guidelines. The basis, which led the court to sift the relevant from the irrelevant, does not become clear from the contents of the judgment.

It is also relevant to note the observation of the apex court to the effect that, '*...and we cannot substitute our view to that of the authorities.*' The observation must be legally sound. After all the authorities have the technical and administrative expertise and their view should not be countered by the judiciary. But a contradiction surfaces when it is applied to my eligibility for the Army Commander's post vis-à-vis one year's experience of command of a Corps. The Army Chief, the Ministry of Defence, the Cabinet Secretary and the ACC itself had found me eligible after the grant of six months waiver. However, despite this, the apex court substituted their view to that of the authorities and found me ineligible on account of a shortfall of 23 days in the required one-year experience. I presume the reader will not disagree with me if I conclude that in my case the Hon'ble Court appear to have substituted their view to that of the authorities in a selective manner.

On the observation of the Hon'ble Court, *'or that the members of the force being aware who is the best is not heading them will certainly weaken the esteem and morale of the force'*, it is indeed laudable and needs to be supported by one and all. The Army must have the best. However, in the instant case, I can only comment that by confining the selection to only two Lt Gens out of a total of nine eligible, then finding one of them (me) ineligible on account of the 23 days shortfall in the required minimum one-year command of a Corps, thus reducing the consideration list to just one name, it cannot be said that the best has been selected to head the force. Therefore, as the Court observed, if the esteem and the morale of the force had to be weakened by the way the Government went about appointing Lt Gen Kalkat, the judgment certainly did not succeed in preventing that from happening. If indeed it is a selection post, as the Court has held, and the best is required to be selected so as to uphold the '*the esteem and morale of the force*' then the ends of justice would have been met only if the Court had asked the Government to reconsider the whole issue and enlarge the list to include all the eligible Lt Gens. Not only that it did not happen in my case, even afterwards the Government has continued to appoint Army Commanders on a single name basis. Even the criteria, that must be laid down if it is a selection post and a comparison is to be carried out, have not been laid down. After removing me from the race, it is business as usual for the Government that continues to follow the seniority-cum-fitness criteria for the post. Can there be anything more discriminatory?

Final Comments: Let me reproduce two of the prayers that formed part of my writ petition:

(a) Issue a writ of certiorari or any other appropriate writ, order or direction calling for the records of the Selection Board held on 31.10.1996 and the decision taken thereon by Respondent no. 1 and after examining the same quashing the deferment of the case of the Petitioner as being arbitrary, unconstitutional and violative of Article 14 of the Constitution of India and further directing that the petitioner be deemed to be promoted to the rank of Lt Gen with effect from 31.10.1996.

(b) Issue a writ of Mandamus and or order or direction calling for records and setting aside the directions of Respondent no. 1 rejecting prayer (a) of the statutory complaint dated 05.10.1997 filed by the Petitioner under Section 27 of the Army Act.

One referred to the arbitrary change of my grading from 'fit' to 'deferred' in the 1996 Selection Board. The other referred to that part of my statutory complaint where I had asked to be deemed to have been placed in command of a

Corps retrospectively (from 31 October 1996) and the government rejecting it on the false ground that I 'must have furnished' adverse career certificate.

The courts have undoubtedly full rights to accept or reject the prayer of a petitioner. However, it is not unreasonable for a petitioner to expect that the grounds and reasons for rejection of his prayer should be spelt out in the judgement. Unfortunately, in the Supreme Court judgement in my case that has not happened. If either of these two prayers had been accepted, it would have had a major bearing on the overall case, and the chapter of my eligibility vis-à-vis one year of command of Corps would have been closed. As it happened both these prayers got dismissed without finding any mention in the apex court judgement.

9

After the Supreme Court Judgement

I received the Supreme Court judgment with a great sense of shock and disbelief. For a few days I could not even read the judgment. Every time I started to read the 32-page judgment I was filled with a rage, the ferocity of which even surprised me. I could not sleep and had difficulty in getting my mind to focus. Negative thoughts of various kinds kept coming into my mind. I felt like shaking the world and bringing the whole system down. I felt utterly cheated and stabbed in the back by my own Chief and by the Government, for which I had given my heart and soul for the last forty years. If they had to decide my career advancement based on extraneous factor, they should have had the courage to look me in the eye and told me so.

While I did not put it beyond the design of the government to meddle into the senior Army appointments for their political gains, I could not understand the rationale behind the apex court arriving at the decision they did. Even if they concluded, from their finding based on *'what was in the mind of the authority'*, that the post of Army Commander was a selection post, how could the highest court ignore or overlook the numerous falsehoods and the irregularities injected into my career profile, the proof of which I submitted to the Court with documentary evidence. How could they conclude that the comparison was a fair one? They had been apprised that ever since they framed the rules in October 1986, there had been dozens of Lt Gens appointed Army Commanders, each one without exception was so appointed based on his seniority–cum–fitness. How could the fact that I had been discriminated against and my fundamental right of equal opportunity had been violated, escape the notice of the apex court? Where was I to seek redress when even the apex court had ignored my plea?

As time passed, disgust began to take the place of anger. I felt sorry that the country for which I had been risking my life was in the hands of politicians who put parochial considerations over principles; that the bureaucrats who form a vital cog in running the country resorted to chicanery and corrupt practices; and worst of all that my blind faith in and unflinching loyalty to the office of the Chief of Army Staff was belied and betrayed by the then incumbent who stooped so low as to perjure himself, bringing down in my esteem the dignity and prestige of the high office he was holding. **There cannot be a greater injury than the breach of faith**.

I realised that inaction was causing me health problems. I had to channel my energy in some direction. I examined my legal options. There is a provision of a Review Petition that can be filed seeking review of the decision of the Supreme Court. As per rules, it has to be filed within thirty days of the announcement of the judgment, goes before the same Hon'ble judges, no fresh facts can be agitated, and there is no hearing. Instead, the Hon'ble members of the Bench take a decision in their chamber. In other words, it merely means requesting the Bench whether they would reconsider what they have already decided a few weeks earlier. *Prima facie* the outcome can be expected to be a rejection of the petition. I do not have statistics but it must have been a rare occasion when the Bench reviewed and changed their own decision.

I consulted my counsel Mr PP Rao on the filing of the review petition. He advised me against it and clearly told me that I would be merely wasting my time and money in doing so, as no positive outcome would be forthcoming. His advice was obviously based on what he had personally witnessed during the proceedings. All the same I filed the review petition on 28 August 2000. As expected it was rejected by a brief order dated 21 September 2000, which read:

> *'Upon perusing the papers, the Court made the following Order*
>
> *The review petitions are dismissed in terms of the signed order.'*

Keeping in mind his high reputation, I sought an interview with the Defence Minister, George Fernandes, which was granted on 14 November 2000. In this interview I apprised him of the continuous discrimination I had been subjected to starting from 1996 when the Ministry had altered my grading from 'fit' to 'deferred' for reasons never conveyed to me. I also showed him all the documentary proof of the falsehoods stated by the Ministry. He gave me a patient hearing and promised that he would do something and get back to me. He never got back to me.

Back to Supreme Court

The Supreme Court judgment was widely reported. One of the persons who read it was Maj Gen KN Misra (Retd). Misra had been the Judge Advocate General of the Army when I filed the writ petition in the Delhi High Court. We had had no personal acquaintance. In mid 2001, after he had retired, we came in contact. He had read the judgment in my case in the *Law Reporter* and asked me what I proposed to do. I told him that I had exhausted all my legal options and there was nothing that I was planning on. He said he had found a clear violation of my fundamental right and urged me to file a petition in the Supreme Court under Article 14 of the Constitution. I readily agreed.

The next problem was to find a lawyer who could be persuaded to take up my case. I contacted several senior lawyers. On reading the judgment all of them agreed that there were errors in the judgment but no one was willing to confront the apex court on the issue. They kept repeating the phrase 'finality of law' implying that a case must reach finality. As the affected party I found difficult to accept this line of argument since they all agreed that there were errors in the judgment since then why could it not be challenged? Their opposition was not on any conceptual grounds but simply because they did not want to annoy the apex court by questioning its judgment, thereby jeopardising their own chances of winning future cases, since they had to practise in the same court. At a human level their reluctance was understandable, as they did not want to hurt their business in any way. Ironically, by implication it also made clear that judgments in the highest court appear to be given based on who is arguing and not necessarily on the merits of the case.

Finally, I found a senior lawyer, Mr Anil Divan, who was bold enough to agree.

I filed my civil writ petition in the Supreme Court in August 2001. In this petition I highlighted the fact that even after the Supreme Court judgment on 28 July 2000, four posts of Army Commander had been filled by appointing the seniormost eligible Lt Gen based on seniority-cum-fitness principle without resorting to comparative merit. I had therefore been discriminated against and sought the intervention of the Hon'ble Court for enforcement of my fundamental right of equal opportunity.

There were some other similar cases where petitions under Article 32 of the Constitution had been filed. The Supreme Court decided to form a Constitution Bench to decide whether a person who had lost the case in the Supreme Court, and whose review petition had also been dismissed, still had a right to go back to the apex court. My writ petition also got linked to that larger issue. One had to await the outcome of the Constitution Bench.

The judgment of the Constitution Bench came on 10 April 2002. The gist of the judgment as given on page 47 of the judgment in case of Rupa Ashok Hurra versus Ashok Hurra & Anr says, ' The upshot of the discussion in our view is that this Court to prevent abuse of its process and to cure a gross miscarriage of justice, may re-consider its judgments in exercise of its inherent power.'

The Hon'ble Bench permitted filing of a curative petition provided that the petitioner establishes, '(1) violation of principles of natural justice in that he was not a party to the lis but the judgment adversely affected his interests or, if he was a party to the lis, he was not served with notice of the proceedings and the matter proceeded as if he had notice and (2) where in the proceedings a learned judge failed to disclose his connection with the subject-matter or the parties giving scope for an apprehension of bias and the judgment adversely affects the petitioner.'

Elsewhere in the judgment there was flexibility in the grounds on which a curative petition may be filed and it was laid down, '*It is neither advisable nor possible to enumerate all the grounds on which such a petition may be entertained.*'

I still did not want to lose any opportunity where I could knock on the doors of the judiciary. Therefore, on 13 August 2002, I filed a curative petition. Relevant extracts of this petition are reproduced below: -

6. *Throughout the history of the Indian Army appointment to the post of Army Commander has always been made based on seniority-cum-fitness. This has been the case not only before the impugned judgment dated 28.7.2000, but also after that. During the hearing of SLP the Govt concealed from the Hon'ble Court an important fact that had a vital bearing on my case. On 02 August 1997 Lt General MR Sharma had filed a statutory complaint. In this he had prayed that while appointing the senior most eligible Lt General HB Kala to the post of Army Commander, being the second in seniority and being eligible and fit, his own profile should be compared with that of Lt Gen Kala. The Govt rejected the complaint. The Petitioner has reason to believe, that as per notings on the files of the Army Headquarters and the Govt, the only ground based on which the Govt rejected the complaint was that the Army Commander's post is a non-selection post. The Govt has thus misled the Hon'ble Court by taking a totally opposite stand in the case of the Petitioner that has resulted in the Petitioner being singled out for discrimination leading to gross miscarriage of justice. This Hon'ble Court may kindly call for the documents for perusal.*

My earlier experience with the apex court had convinced me that they would not accede to my request of calling for documents. Therefore, I gave statistical logic that the government, having singled me out for discrimination continued to make appointments based on the principle of seniority-cum-fitness.

This is what I wrote in paragraph 7 of my curative petition:

7. *'It is humbly submitted that even after the impugned judgment on 28.7.2000, six Lt Generals were appointed Army Commanders during 2000 and 2001 (List attached as Annexure P-IV). In each case without exception the*

senior most eligible Lt general has been appointed Army Commander. That these six were appointed based on the principle of seniority-cum-fitness can even be proved statistically and logically. For each of these six vacancies, as and when these occurred, all the six senior most Lt Generals were eligible. In the Petitioner's case, out of a total of nine eligible Lt Generals, only the two senior most officers had been considered and their career profile was compared. Assuming that the Govt has followed the same norm for the subsequent six appointments, then, for the first vacancy, No 1 and No 2 in seniority would have been compared. Since No 1 was appointed, he must have been found higher in merit than No 2. For the next vacancy since No 2 was appointed Army Commander, he must have been found to be higher than No 3. Similarly, down the line, when No 6 was appointed, he was lower in merit than No 5, who in turn was lower than No 4, who himself had been lower than No 3 and so on. Therefore, if the Govt was indeed treating the post of Army Commander as a selection post, then statistically, since senior most eligible officer has always been appointed (with the sole exception of the Petitioner), every new Army Commander is lower in merit than his predecessor. That would mean that as time passes the Govt has been lowering the standards for appointing officers to the senior Army post of Army Commander. This can be neither logical nor true. The fact is that the post of Army Commander is a non-selection post which has always been filled based on principle of seniority-cum-fitness. The criteria for the appointment are laid down in Govt of India letter No 13684/JS/(P&W)/86 dated 20.10.1986, copy of which is hereto marked and annexed as Annexure P V. Only the Petitioner has been singled out for discrimination in gross violation of the principle of natural justice.

The apex court rejected the curative petition in November 2002, more than two months after I had retired from the Army. In the order rejecting the petition there was of course no mention of the points that I had raised therein. There was no mention whether my fundamental right of equal opportunity was violated or not.

I tried my best to get the Supreme Court to reopen the case in view of the factual inaccuracies in their judgment and all the facts being overwhelmingly in my favour. I failed to persuade the Hon'ble members of the judiciary to reconsider the judgment. It is not that such revision of an earlier decision has never been done. But I did not have the luck of an AR Antulay.

A Reference to the Human Rights Commission

Since the denial of right of equal opportunity is a violation of human rights, I decided to approach the Human Rights Commission. I wrote to them on 21 February 2004 thus:

To,

Dr. AS Anand

Chairman National Human Rights Commission

Sardar Patel Bhawan

Sansad Marg, New Delhi – 110 002

Sir,

I have the honour to state that I am happy to learn that under your chairmanship the Human Rights Commission has been taking a very proactive stance in protecting communities, classes and individuals from human rights abuses. I am also approaching you for the same purpose.

I retired from the Army on 31 August 2002 as a Lt Gen. While in service, based on the policy as well as the precedent of the Central Govt, I should have been appointed an Army Commander on 1 March 1998. However, making an unprecedented departure from its own norms, the Govt denied me that post and a junior was appointed instead. Supersessions in the Army, especially at such high levels, are a very serious matter because they reflect on the worth of a commander in the eyes of his troops whose respect and confidence is essential for him to win and retain if he were to command them in any viable and effective manner. Since my supersession was without any justification or basis and was in fact unprecedented in the entire history of the Indian Army, I challenged it in Delhi High Court. I won the case with the single judge and the appeal with the Division Bench in that Court. However, the Govt went into an SLP and I lost the case in the Supreme Court in July 2000. You may not remember but you had in fact delivered the judgment.

It transpired after the judgment that the Govt had misrepresented a critical fact to the court in order to obtain a judgment in its favour. In its arguments the Govt had pleaded that the post of Army Commander is a selection post and thus the Govt had a right to exercise its prerogative to make a selection between those that met the criteria for appointment. Subsequently, after the judgment, it came to light that in an earlier case, where Lt Gen MR Sharma, the then Deputy Chief of Army Staff (Training and Coordination), had filed a statutory complaint on 2 August 1997 to the Govt of India claiming consideration of his name for the Army Commander's post along with his senior Lt Gen HB Kala, the same Govt had rejected his complaint taking the grounds that the post of Army Commander is a non-selection post and has to be given to the senior most officer eligible for the post. The Govt concealed this fact from the court during hearings in my case, which enabled it to take a totally opposite stance and obtain a decision in its favour.

On learning of this, I filed a fresh appeal in July 2001 in the Supreme Court requesting for enforcement of my fundamental right of equal opportunity. There were a few brief hearings but the case got mired in technical points related to my legal right to seek review of the case. The point about misrepresentation of a material fact by the Govt or violation of my fundamental right was never discussed.

After the Supreme Court dismissed my appeal in July 2000, giving a judgment that the post of Army Commander being a selection post, the Govt has a right to make a selection amongst eligible officers, the Govt has continued to appoint Army Commanders based on the old principle of seniority-cum-fitness. Over a dozen Army Commanders have been thus appointed till date. All of them, without exception, were the seniormost and have been appointed based on their fitness and seniority. What is more, the Govt has not laid down even the norms for comparison, which is a minimum necessity if a selection is to be made, leave aside carrying out any actual comparison among eligible officers. In fact in the entire history of the Indian Army, at least since 1947, no officer has ever been superseded by a junior for the post of an Army Commander if he was graded fit for promotion and was medically fit, except me. I have thus been singled out for discrimination and have been denied my right of equal opportunity and have been made to live a life of indignity and dishonour implying that I was somehow not actually fit even though I was so graded.

I am not a legal person. My entire exposure to the law before this case was limited to administering simple

Army justice as a commander. I had always administered it with a firm belief that the sole purpose of the law is to administer justice and the latter must take precedence over any law, let alone over legal procedures and nuances, always and every time. And, here is a straightforward case, an open and shut case if you may, where the Govt has accepted that I was fully eligible based on their own criteria, and no senior who was eligible has ever been superseded in the entire history of the Indian Army whether before or after my case. Also, it does not appear that the Govt superseded me because it did not like me or had anything against me personally simply because it appointed me a Deputy Chief of Army Staff at Army Headquarters soon after my legal challenge had run its course. The only motive had to be to appoint Lt Gen Kalkat an Army Commander, who because of his impending superannuation could not be so appointed without superseding me. It did not matter who was in Kalkat's way at that time; it could have been anyone else for that matter. As a responsible person, it would be wrong on my part to deliberate on that motive beyond saying that it had nothing to do with professional service, institutional or national interests or considerations and that fact is universally known throughout the Army. The fact that the Govt could succeed in misleading the Supreme Court itself is especially painful. I find it hard to accept that in a democracy like ours, which is an envy of at least the entire Third World, there is no accountability or remedy against such a conduct by the Govt or those who happened to be representing it at a certain time.

In view of the circumstances explained above, I request your honour as Chairman of the Human Rights Commission to intervene now and take whatever steps you consider appropriate to salvage my honour and restore my right of equal opportunity so that I do not have to live the rest of my life in indignity. Your Commission has already set a laudable precedent in this respect in the case of Shri Prakash Singh Badal, ex Chief Minister of Punjab, who had approached it for protection against what he perceived as harassment by the Punjab Govt, by asking the latter to submit a report to the Commission. I pray that the Commission provide me a similar protection and ask the Central Govt to report to it as to why it misled the Supreme Court by stating that the appointment of the Army Commander is based on selection whereas it had taken an opposite stand in an earlier case.

I do hope and pray that my appeal to your Commission is not looked at differently just because I have no political clout, unlike Shri Badal, but am just an ordinary citizen of the country who had served it to the best of my humble ability.

If you so desire, I will consider it a privilege to appear before your commission and give it fuller details of the case.

Awaiting a favourable response.

Sd.....
21 Feb 2004

The Commission wrote back on 25 May 2004 to say:

The Commission of complaint dated 21/02/2004 in respect of Lt.Gen. R. S. KADYAN has passed the following order on 01/04/2004.

The complaint is not entertainable in accordance with the provision of Section 36 of the Protection of Human Rights Act 1993 read with Regulation 9 of the National Human rights Commission (Procedure) Regulations 1994, as amended. Hence, no action is called for and file is closed.

I do not know what the quoted section states. I only know that truth has always been in my favour. When the law was in my favour, the non-legal factor of morale was brought in. Now, when the Constitution gives me the right of equality, some section of law is held against me.

Prosecution of Government Officials

When the High Court judgment came out on 11 December 1998, from its contents I had learnt of the falsehoods stated by various government functionaries at different stages. I decided to prosecute them. Since the individuals had committed these offences while acting in the discharge of their duties, I had to seek sanction of the government in terms of Section 197 (1) and (2) of Criminal procedure Code, 1973, for prosecuting them. I sought that permission vide my application dated 3 April 2001 addressed to the Central Government and forwarded 'through proper channel'. In this I had named the following officials:

(a) TSR Subramanian, the Cabinet Secretary, for falsifying my official records in the Note put up by him to the Prime Minister. It is my belief that either the Ministry of Defence or the Military Secretary under orders of the Army Chief would have introduced the falsehoods in my profile. However, since the only documentary proof I have is a copy of the Note dated 27 Mar 1998 signed by the Cabinet secretary, I included his name.

(b) General (Retd) VP Malik, the then COAS for misleading the Defence Minister by stating in his note dated 6 Mar 1998 that Lt Generals IJ Khanna, Maya Dass and GL Bakshi, though senior most were not appointed Army Commanders because of comparative merit. Secondly, for misleading the Delhi High Court by falsely stating in his affidavit dated 17 July 1998 that he had recommended Kalkat's name for the appointment as per existing guidelines, well knowing that there are no rules, orders or guidelines other than the Govt letter dated 20 Oct 1986.

(c) Shri RK Kalia, the then Under Secretary in the Ministry of Defence, for making two false statements in the affidavit in the SLP in the Supreme Court. Firstly (in relation to my posting to Paris) he stated that I 'gave requisite willingness in accordance with the OM stated therein...' well knowing no such willingness was given by me. Secondly, he falsely stated that I 'got my tenure extended for about 21 months ...' well knowing that my repatriation was delayed in organisational interests and I had no hand in getting it extended.

(d) Shri AJS Sahney, Director (MS), Ministry of Defence (he had signed the Government order granting me waiver) for rejecting my main prayer in the statutory complaint on the false pretext that I 'must have furnished adverse career certificate,' well knowing that no such certificate had been furnished.

I must confess that I have nothing personal against these officials. In fact apart from Gen Malik I haven't even met the others. I quoted their names because the documents where my record had been falsified are signed by them.

Till date there has been no response from the government despite reminders sent by me. In any case the government was not expected to grant me permission to prosecute bureaucrats for doing the government bidding. However, their silence despite my reminders was adequate basis for me to go to court for their prosecution. However, ultimately I dropped the idea of doing so. I took that decision, not because I did not have documentary proof of their falsehoods, but simply because by now I had lost hope of getting a fair judgment from the judiciary in a matter related to this case.

10

Let There be Competition

The reader might have gathered an impression that I had been harping only on my seniority and was scared of competition. Such an impression would be erroneous. I have never laid claim that I have been the best General in the Indian Army. However, with all humility I can say – and with certainty - that I have all along been higher than Kalkat in merit. Through doctoring of my profile and through manipulation by the concerned officials it has been made to appear that I was lower than Kalkat in comparative merit. It has only added insult to injury. If the Army Chief and the government wanted it to be treated as a selection post, so be it. However, that comparison should have been fairly and objectively conducted instead of being manipulated merely to arrive at a pre-determined conclusion. Let me give some facts in support of my claim that I stood higher than Kalkat in merit at various stages of our service.

To start at the beginning, I passed out of the National Defence Academy holding the highest appointment of Academy Cadet Captain and winning the President's Gold Medal for being adjudged the all round best cadet of the course and the Silver Medal for standing first in the overall order of merit. Kalkat was not even given a permanent appointment (out of a total of 38 such appointments, which were given by merit) during the final term. When we were commissioned from the Indian Military Academy, I passed out at the third position in the entire course. Kalkat was at 43rd position.

In late eighties and early nineties the MS Branch had tried a system of transparency. Every officer was allowed to walk into the computer room of this Branch and obtain the following information:

(a) One's own Overall Average Performance (OAP) in terms of a figure out of a maximum of 9. The figure of '9' corresponds to the 'outstanding' grading in the Army and is the highest that can be awarded.

(b) The Average OAP of the top 10 officers of the batch. In the case of Kalkat and me this meant all officers commissioned in the calendar year 1962. Since in 1962 three courses had been commissioned instead of the normal two (as a result of the war with China), the total number of officers in the batch could have been 1200 to 1500.

(c) The OAP of the bottom 10 officers of the batch.

I checked the data during April 1990 when both of us were holding the rank of Brigadier. The details were:

(a) My overall OAP – 8.13

(b) Overall OAP of the top 10 officers of our batch – 8.13

(c) Overall OAP of the bottom 10 officers of our batch – 5.70

Since my OAP was the same as the OAP of the top ten officers of the batch, simple arithmetic would prove that my position in merit could be as high as number 1, or, the lowest it could go down to was number 5 or 6.

What was Kalkat's OAP? Let me not breach confidentiality of a colleague's records. I will only give other indicators.

In Nov 1989 the Army, during their selection of Military Attaché for Paris, took out a merit list of top 20 Brigadiers. I was at number 1 position in this list. Kalkat's name did not even figure in this list of the first 20.

Whenever a selection board is convened, the MS Branch draws up an 'Internal Batch Assessment' (IBA) to facilitate the working of the selection board. The IBA is prepared purely on the basis of merit and covers overall career profile of all concerned officers of a particular batch. When our batch came up for consideration for promotion to the rank of Lt Gen by Special Selection Board, in the IBA prepared up till and inclusive of the rank of Maj Gen, I was above Kalkat. This can be proved by a simple historical fact.

When our batch was considered for promotion to the rank of Lt Gen, it is a matter of record that I was graded 'fit' by the Selection Board, whereas Kalkat was graded 'unfit'. This leaves no doubt that based on the record up to and inclusive of Maj Gen, I was higher than him in merit. He got his promotion to the rank of Lt Gen through a statutory complaint. Of this complaint too, the Army Chief had recommended rejection; but he was overruled by the Ministry, who accepted Kalkat's complaint and promoted him to the rank of Lt Gen.

The above would make it clear that up to and inclusive of the rank of Maj Gen I was higher than Kalkat in the overall merit. After promotion to the rank of Lt Gen, the ACR form does not include any numerical grades, which could permit comparison. Therefore, our relative merit, drawn up as we were getting promoted from Maj Gen to Lt Gen could not have undergone any change. Further, after promotion to the rank of Lt Gen I was awarded the Ati Vishisht Seva Medal by the President on 26 January 1998. This would have further pushed up my merit even higher, and this input was available when we were considered for the appointment of Army Commander.

The strongest point I have to prove that I was higher in merit vis-à-vis Kalkat, is the fact that the Army and the Government had to resort to numerous falsehoods and distortions of my profile to somehow concoct that Kalkat was more suited for the appointment of Army Commander. A lie is resorted to when truth is inadequate to prove a point. If the comparison was carried out in a fair and just manner with an open mind, I never had any doubt that I stood way above Kalkat. However, what was done was not comparison but a farce of comparison to justify a pre-determined decision. The records are still there. Let any neutral agency undertake the task. But who will and why?

If it is intended that even after one has gone through five selection boards, there is a need to compare profiles for the appointment of Army Commanders, so be it. But as a starter, the minimum requirement is for the Government to lay down a criterion for such comparison and announce it to all, just as it has been done for all the five selection boards. It cannot be left to the individual fancy of certain individuals. Till date no such criterion exists.

It is also relevant to clarify the concept of seniority in the Army. The inter se seniority of officers of a batch is not decided by first-cum-first-served basis or by any arbitrary method. The seniority is determined by the order of merit at the time of being commissioned as officers. If I was senior to Kalkat, it was because I was placed higher than him in merit after four years of training as cadets in the Academy. My seniority was not gifted to me; I earned it the hard way.

Other Side Effects of Challenging the System

An Army officer is generally not fully conversant with his own pay and entitlements. In 1999 when we were deployed along the borders during Operation Vijay, a knowledgeable colleague brought an anomaly to my notice. Due to my delayed repatriation from Paris, I was promoted to the rank of Maj Gen in September 1995, three years behind my juniors. Similarly, I was promoted Lt Gen in October 1997 clearly two years after my juniors were promoted. Whereas I was given my original seniority in the respective rank (I was the senior most infantry officer of the entire 1962 batch) immediately on promotion, my pay was fixed at the bottom of that rank and was lower than being drawn by my juniors. As a result, both as a Maj Gen and as an Lt Gen I continued getting salary that was lower than given to those who were my junior. This disparity also gets reflected in pension (which is related to the last pay drawn) and is carried into one's entire life span. This was not in order. After writing to the Controller of Defence Accounts (Officers) and subsequently to the Adjutant General, and not getting a satisfactory reply, I filed a statutory complaint with the Central Government on 17 August 2000. In this single page complaint, after giving the necessary background, I made the following prayer:

"(a) My salary may kindly be fixed in such a manner that at no stage should I have got salary lower than my juniors of the same cadre and holding the same rank. More specifically my pay as Major General from 3 September 1995 to 30 September 1997 and my pay as a Lieutenant General from 1 October 1997 till date may please be re-fixed so that it is not lower at any stage during this period than my juniors holding the same rank.

(b) After refixation, all the arrears due to me from 3 September 1995 onwards may kindly be paid to me."

As per existing rules, a statutory complaint must be finally disposed of by the government within 9 months. However, in my case, despite reminders, the complaint was kept pending till I retired on 31 August 2002, more than two years after it was filed. When nothing was heard, in December 2002, I wrote a personal letter to the Defence Minister, Shri George Fernades. In this I stated that I was not seeking any special favours but was only asking for my due as per the government's 'one below rule'. Under this rule if a junior is promoted ahead of a senior, the latter is automatically brought on a higher pay scale. I again wrote to him in November 2003. I never received a reply from the Defence Minister, not even an acknowledgement. Till date my statutory complaint remains pending.

If the Government found that I had no case, they should have rejected my complaint. Their silence is intriguing. One can only infer that they have something to hide. It is also making a mockery of the rules by simply not responding to a complaint.

Conclusion

My not becoming an Army Commander hurt a lot, both on personal and professional levels. On the first because it was so patently unjust and unfair and on the second because it was Eastern Command. I was particularly keen on Eastern Command, responsible for the North-East where the biggest threat is insurgency. I wanted to apply the lessons I had imbibed during my long innings in Nagaland and Mizoram to insurgencies in Assam and Manipur.

The bureaucracy of the MoD was lined up by Kalkat in his corner ever since they promoted him to Lt Gen against the recommendations of the Army Selection Board and the Chief of the Army Staff. They indulged in every trick in their huge arsenal to promote his intersts. Politicians are what they are despite their chest thumping, but what hurt most was the Army Chief bending with the wind. The big shock was the Supreme Court. Was it that it was reluctant to embarrass the government, or was it afraid to take on the responsibility of interfering in the internal functioning of the MoD/Army in case of what the government repeatedly kept calling a 'sensitive' appointment? Or was it afraid of undermining that least-understood but most misused world called 'morale'? Or were some other factors at work?

Yet some good must come out of my experience. I believe the bureaucrats are the worst link in the chain and most times they fire the gun off the shoulders of the politicians without the latter even being aware of it. I am convinced that the bureaucrats must be kept out of the promotions and appointments of the defence forces. How that can be accomplished in a responsible manner and who should excercise over-right in the Services promotion boards is beyond the scope of this book and is a matter that needs to be studied in greater details by subject matter experts. Perhaps, a study team consisting of retired Service Chiefs and Military Secretaries assisted by a retired judge should be formed to analyse the matter in depth and to come up with a process that is just, fair, open and transparent. Once so established, the process must be implemented without exceptions, 'special cases' or other deviations. Will that make the system perfect or fail-safe? No, a process or system can be only as good as people running it. But will it improve what is in place today? The answer is a resounding year; anything will.

Index